The  POCKETGuide
ITALY

Original text by Jane Shaw
Updated by Sally Roy

© Automobile Association Developments Limited 2008
First published 2008

ISBN: 978-0-7495-5518-4

Published by AA Publishing, a trading name of Automobile Association Developments Limited, whose registered office is Fanum House, Basing View, Basingstoke, Hampshire RG21 4EA. Registered number 1878835.

Automobile Association Developments Limited retains the copyright in the original edition © 1999 and in all subsequent editions, reprints and amendments

A CIP catalogue record for this book is available from the British Library

Colour separation: Keenes, Andover
Printed and bound in Italy by Printer Trento S.r.l.

Front cover images: (t) AA/C Sawyer; (b) AA/T Souter
Back cover image: AA/C Sawyer

A03404
Maps in this title produced from map data © 1998 – 2005 Navigation Technologies BV. All rights reserved
Transport map © Communicarta Ltd, UK

About this book

Symbols are used to denote the following categories:

✚ map reference

✉ address or location

☎ telephone number

🕐 opening times

✋ admission charge

🍴 restaurant or café on premises
or nearby

Ⓜ nearest underground train station

🚌 nearest bus/tram route

🚃 nearest overground train station

⛴ nearest ferry stop

ℹ tourist information office

❷ other practical information

↔ other places of interest nearby

➤ indicates the page where you will
find a fuller description

This book is divided into four sections.

Planning pages 6–19
Before You Go; Getting There; Getting
Around; Being There

Best places to see pages 20–41
The unmissable highlights of any visit
to Italy

Exploring pages 42–127
The best places to visit in Italy,
organized by area

Maps pages 131–144
All map references are to the atlas
section. For example, Ravenna has the
reference ✚ 133 E7 – indicating the
page number and grid square in which it
is to be found

Contents

Planning

Before You Go

WHEN TO GO

JAN	FEB	MAR	APR	MAY	JUN	JUL	AUG	SEP	OCT	NOV	DEC
7°C	8°C	11°C	14°C	18°C	23°C	26°C	25°C	22°C	18°C	13°C	9°C
45°F	46°F	52°F	57°F	64°F	73°F	79°F	77°F	72°F	64°F	55°F	48°F

High season   Low season

Italy's climate ranges from Alpine in the mountains of the far north and scorching hot and dry in the most southerly areas. The central section is more variable, with summer temperatures often exceeding 30°C (86°F) and consistent sunshine during the day. The hottest months are July to September, and at this time humidity is boosted by the hot Sirocco wind blowing up from Africa. Overnight temperatures can also be very high, and city residents (particularly Romans) tend to head for the coast and countryside.

In winter, the north becomes a winter-sports playground, while the rest of the country – even the south – is often plagued by rain and fog and can be bitterly cold. Venice is prone to flooding, and so are some other areas.

WHAT YOU NEED

● Required
○ Suggested
▲ Not required

Some countries require a passport to remain valid for a minimum period (usually at least six months) beyond the date of entry – contact their consulate or embassy or your travel agent for details.

	UK	Germany	USA	Netherlands	Spain
Passport (or National Identity Card where applicable)	●	●	●	●	▲
Visa (regulations can change – check before you travel)	▲	▲	▲	▲	▲
Onward or Return Ticket	▲	▲	▲	▲	▲
Health Inoculations (tetanus and polio)	▲	▲	▲	▲	▲
Health Documentation (► 9, Health Advice)	●	●	▲	●	●
Travel Insurance	○	○	○	○	○
Driving Licence (national)	●	●	●	●	●
Car Insurance Certificate	●	●	●	●	●
Car Registration Document	●	●	●	●	●

ADVANCE PLANNING
WEBSITES
- **www.**enit.it (the site of the Italian State Tourist Office)
- **www.**italiantourism.com (a site especially for visitors from the US)
- **www.**romaturismo.it (the website of the Rome tourist office)
- **www.**museionline.it (the official site for state and other museums across Italy. Opening times and admission prices are not always up to date, but the background (English version available) is useful
- **www.**firenze.net (the best Florence website)
- **www.**trenitalia.it (for booking Italy's excellent rail system)

TOURIST OFFICES
In the UK
Italian State Tourist Board
✉ 1 Princes Street, London W1R 8AY ☎ 020 7408 1254; **www.**enit.it

In the USA
Italian State Tourist Board
✉ 630 Fifth Avenue, Suite 1565, New York NY 10111 ☎ 212/245-4822; **www.**italiantourism.com

Italian State Tourist Board
✉ 12400 Wilshire Boulevard Suite 550, Los Angeles CA 90025 ☎ 310/820-1898; **www.**italiantourism.com

HEALTH ADVICE
Insurance Nationals of EU countries receive reduced cost medical (including hospital and dental) treatment within the Italian health service and pay a percentage for prescribed medicines. You need a European Health Insurance Card (EHIC). Private medical insurance is still advised. US visitors should check their insurance coverage.

TIME DIFFERENCES

GMT 12 noon	Italy 1PM	Germany 1PM	USA (NY) 7AM	Netherlands 1PM	Spain 1PM

Italy is one hour ahead of Greenwich Mean Time (GMT+1), but from late March, when clocks are put forward one hour, to late October, Italian Summer Time (GMT+2) operates.

WHAT'S ON WHEN

Saints' Days The events listed below are only a few of the traditional holidays and feast days that are celebrated in Italy. Most communities also have religious parades on their patron saint's day, when effigies and relics of the saint and/or Virgin are taken in procession from the main church and paraded through the streets by priests, nuns, monks and pilgrims, often in historic costume. They usually finish at some significant spot (often in or by the sea in coastal communities) and are followed by general celebrations.

January *New Year's Day:* public holiday.
Epiphany (6 Jan): public holiday. Traditionally the *befana* (witch) leaves presents for children.

February Week leading up to Shrove Tuesday: *Carnevale.* Streets full of adults and children in fancy dress throwing confetti and firecrackers. Particularly important in Venice.

March/April *Good Friday:* Pope leads ceremony of the Stations of the Cross at the Colosseum in Rome (➤ 30–31).
Easter Sunday: Papal address from San Pietro (➤ 22–23).
Settimana Beni Culturali (Late Mar–early Apr): a week of free admission and guided tours to state museums and other, infrequently open, monuments.
Rome's birthday (21 Apr): music all over the city and fireworks at night.
Liberation Day (25 Apr): public holiday. Commemorates the Allies' liberation of Italy from the Nazis in 1944.
Maggio Musicale Fiorentino, Firenze (late Apr): Classical music, dance and opera festival, featuring world-class performers and conductors.

May *Labour Day* (1 May): public holiday.
Festa dei Ceri, Gubbio (15 May): (➤ 86–87).

June *Calcio Storico Fiorentino* (24 Jun): costume procession,

NATIONAL HOLIDAYS

JAN	FEB	MAR	APR	MAY	JUN	JUL	AUG	SEP	OCT	NOV	DEC
2		1	1	1		1				1	3

1 January	New Year's Day
6 January	Epiphany
March/April	Easter Monday
25 April	Liberation Day, 1945
1 May	Labour Day
15 August	Assumption of the Virgin
1 November	All Saints' Day
8 December	Immaculate Conception
25 December	Christmas Day
26 December	St Stephen's Day

Banks, businesses and most shops and museums close on these days. Most cities, towns and villages celebrate their patron saint's day, but generally, most places remain open.

fireworks and a ball game in Piazza della Signoria, Florence.

July
Palio delle Contrade, Siena (2 Jul): Costumed participants take part in flag-waving and a fearsome bareback horse-race round Piazza del Campo.
Festa della Santa Maria del Carmine, Naples (16 Jul): Historic festival featuring illumination of the church of Santa Maria del Carmine.

August *Ferragosto* (15 Aug): public holiday. Many businesses close for a week or more.
Palio delle Contrade (16 Aug): see 2 July.

Giostra del Saracino, Arezzo (last Sun in Aug): medieval joust.

September *Regata Storica*, Venice (first Sun in Sep): a colourful procession of historic boats and a gondola race.

November *All Saints' Day* (1 Nov): public holiday.

December *Immaculate Conception* (8 Dec): public holiday.
Christmas Day (25 Dec): public holiday. Papal address at San Pietro (► 22–23).
New Year's Eve (31 Dec): fireworks, free concerts and massive *cenone* (dinners) in many restaurants.

Getting There

BY AIR

There are direct flights from Europe and North America to Italy's major international airports.

Rome's main airport is Leonardo da Vinci (known as Fiumicino) ☎ 06 65 951; **www**.adr.it, which is 32km (20 miles) from the centre of Rome. The journey takes 30–45 minutes by the express rail service to Stazione Termini, 50 minutes by bus, and 40 minutes by car. The other airport serving Rome (mostly for charter and cheap flights) is Ciampino (☎ 06 794941; **www**.adr.it), 15km (9 miles) to the southeast. The journey time by road is 30–45 minutes, but there are no direct bus routes into Rome, only links to out-of-city stations.

Milan has two airports, Internazionale Linate and Intercontinentale della Malpensa. For both: ☎ 02 7485 2200; **www**.sea-aeroportimilano.it. Linate airport is 7km (4 miles) from the centre of Milan, with a journey time of 30–40 minutes by bus and 15 minutes by car. Malpensa airport is 50km (31 miles) northwest of Milan, with a journey time of 40 minutes by train to Milano Nord station, 45–60 minutes by shuttle bus, 35–60 minutes by car.

Venice's Marco Polo Airport (☎ 041 260 9260; **www**.veniceairport.it) is 7km (4 miles) from the city by boat across the lagoon, or 12km (7.5 miles) by road. Water taxis get you to the city in 20–35 minutes, land taxis to Piazzale Roma take 15–25 minutes.

Florence and Pisa are served by Galileo Galilei Airport (☎ 050 849300; **www**.pisa-airport.com), located at Pisa, 91km (57 miles) west of Florence. The journey by car into Pisa takes around 5 minutes; Florence is just over an hour away by road.

BY RAIL

Travellers from Britain can take the Eurostar service to Paris or Brussels, from where there are direct trains to Rome, Florence, Milan, Turin and Venice. Most of the Rome services take you to Stazione Termini, the city's main transport hub, but some long-distance services go to Ostiense or Tiburtina, both on the edge of the city. The journey time from London (Waterloo) to Italy is between 11 and 15 hours, depending on your destination, and sleepers are available from Paris.

BY SEA

Ferries from Greece land at Ancona, Bari and Venice. Travellers heading for Sicily will find regular ferry crossings from Naples, Reggio di Calabria and Genoa; for Sardinia, there are ferries from Genoa, Livorno and Civitavecchia.

BY ROAD

Every land route into Italy from the rest of Europe crosses the Alps via one of the passes or tunnels (St Gotthard, Great St Bernard, Frejus and Mont Blanc). From the Channel routes head south through France,

Switzerland and Germany. There are toll roads along the way, and the journey to the Italian border from northern France will take between 11 and 14 hours.

DRIVING

Drive on the right.

Speed limit on motorways *(autostrade)*, which have tolls **130kph (80mph)**; on main roads **110kph (68mph)**; on secondary roads **90kph (56mph)**; on urban roads **50kph (31mph)**.

Seat belts must be worn in front seats at all times and in rear seats where available.

Random breath-testing takes place. Never drive under the influence of alcohol.

Petrol *(benzina)* is expensive. All garages sell unleaded *(senza piombo)* – 95 and 98 octane, diesel *(gasolio)* and liquified petroleum gas (LPG). Outside urban areas filling stations open 7–12.30 and 3–7.30. Motorway services open 24 hours. Credit cards aren't widely accepted away from urban areas. Many automatic pumps take banknotes in denominations of €5, €10 and €20, but may reject older ones.

In the event of a breakdown, ☎ 116, giving your registration number and type of car, and the nearest ACI (Automobile Club d'Italia) office will assist you. This service is free to foreign-registered vehicles or cars rented from Rome or Milan airports (you will need to present your passport).

Getting Around

PUBLIC TRANSPORT

INTERNAL FLIGHTS

Services throughout the country are provided by Alitalia (☎ 06 65 643; **www.**alitalia.com). A more limited list of destinations is offered by Meridiana (☎ 199 207 080) and Air One (☎ 848 848 880 – toll free).

TRAINS

Italian State Railways (Ferrovie dello Stato, or FS; **www.**fs-on-line.com) has an efficient (if slightly confusing) range of services. Regionale, Diretto and Espresso trains stop at every station; Intercity trains cost more but are faster; and the Pendolino is the fastest and most expensive.

LONG-DISTANCE BUSES

There is no national bus company but Eurolines (☎ 055 357 110; **www.**eurolines.com) offers a service between the main Italian towns and several cities outside Italy. Each major city has its own companies for short-, medium- and some long-distance coach travel.

FERRIES

Genoa and Naples are the main ports for the Mediterranean, with regular services to Sicily and Sardinia (**www.**traghettonionline. net/eng). Naples also has services to Capri and other islands, including fast hydrofoils during the height of the summer season. On the Adriatic, Brindisi and Otranto are well served by ferries to Greece. Book well in advance for car ferries. The Italian Lakes, in the north of the country, also have ferries between the towns around their shores. Venice has a comprehensive network of water transport, including *vaporetti* and the faster *motoscafi*, following fixed routes along the canals and the lagoon. At several points along the Grand Canal, gondola-ferries offer a cross-canal service.

URBAN TRANSPORT

Buses are the best way to get around towns of any size. Bus stops *(fermate)* are clearly marked with the routes. You need a ticket before boarding at the rear *(entrata),* where you stamp it in the machine. Exit through the middle door *(uscita).* Some cities have trams, which run like buses. Venice has water buses *(vaporetti),* and Milan and Rome have underground trains. Tickets for urban public

transport can be bought in
tobacconists and newsstands.

TAXIS

Taxis can be hailed in the street,
found at taxi stands (stations and
major *piazze*), or reserved by
telephone. There's an initial charge
and a rate per kilometre. Heavy
traffic can mean stiff meter
increases and there are Sunday and
late-night supplements. In Venice,
there are water taxis, which are
white and have a cabin.

CAR RENTAL

Car rental is available at airports,
main railway stations and town-
centre offices. Small local firms
offer the best rates, but cars can
only be rented locally. Air and train
travellers can book inclusive deals.
To rent a car you need to be over 21
(some companies have a minimum
age of 25) and have held a full
licence for a year. Most of the
major international rental
companies will let you return the
vehicle to another Italian city
(possibly even to other countries),
but ask in advance.

CONCESSIONS

Students/youths Holders of an
International Student Identity Card
(ISIC) and, for those under 26, an
International Youth Card (IYC) can
get discounts on transport,
accommodation, museum entrance
fees, car rental and in restaurants.
Nationals (under 18) of EU and
certain other countries receive free
admission to state museums.
Senior citizens Citizens over the
age of 65 from EU and other
countries with which Italy has a
reciprocal arrangement (not
including the USA) may get free
admission to some museums and
receive discounts at others, as well
as on public transport on production
of their passport.

Being There

TOURIST OFFICES

Most towns or villages have their own small tourist office or Pro Loco with maps and information leaflets. The main cities are listed below.

Florence ✉ Via Cavour 1 ☎ 055 290 832; **www.**firenzeturismo.it

Genoa ✉ Stazione Principe ☎ 01 246 2633; **www.**apt.genova.it

Milan ✉ Palazzo del Turismo, Via Marconi 1 ☎ 02 7252 4301; **www.**milanoinfotourist.com

Naples ✉ Piazza dei Martiri 58 ☎ 081 405 311; **www.**naples.it

Palermo ✉ Piazza Castelnuovo 34/35 ☎ 091 583 847; **www.**palermotourism.com

Rome ✉ Via Parigi 5 ☎ 06 4889 9253; **www.**romaturismo.it
There are information kiosks near many of the main tourist sights.

Turin ✉ Piazza Castello 161 ☎ 011 535 901, 011 535 181; **www.**turismotorino.org

Venice ✉ Piazza San Marco 71/F ☎ 041 529 8711; **www.**turismovenezia.it

EMBASSIES AND CONSULATES

UK ☎ 06 4220 0001; **www.**britain.it
Germany ☎ 06 492 131; **www.**ambgermania.it
USA ☎ 06 46 741; **www.**usembassy.it
Netherlands ☎ 06 332 1141; **www.**olanda.it
Spain ☎ 06 684 0401; **www.**amba-spagna.com

TELEPHONES

Almost every bar has a telephone, and there are many in public places. Most operate with phonecards (*schede telefoniche*), which can be bought from tobacconists, shops, bars, post offices, newsstands and other public places. Some take coins of 10, 20 or 50 cents, €1 or €2, and some take credit cards.

EMERGENCY TELEPHONE NUMBERS

Police 113
Carabinieri 112
Fire 115

OPENING HOURS

- Shops
- Offices
- Banks
- Museums/Monuments
- Churches
- Pharmacies

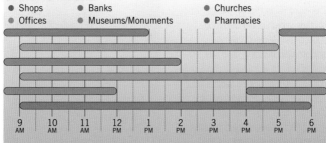

9 AM	10 AM	11 AM	12 PM	1 PM	2 PM	3 PM	4 PM	5 PM	6 PM

Shop opening hours are changing, with shops open until later in the evening, and more all-day and Sunday openings, especially in the main cities and tourist centres. Generally, however, it is Mon–Sat, with a break from 1 to 5pm. Food shops close on Thursday afternoon and others on Monday morning

(plus Saturday afternoon during the summer). Some banks are open until 2pm and close in the afternoon. Many museums now open in the afternoon (5–7.30pm), others are open all day, and a few open late into the evening. Many museums close around 1pm on Sun, and most are closed Mon.

Any emergency (including Ambulance) 118
Road Assistance (ACI) 116

INTERNATIONAL DIALLING CODES

From Italy to:
UK: 00 44
Germany: 00 49
USA/Canada: 00 1
Netherlands: 00 31

POSTAL SERVICES

Rome's main post office is on Piazza San Silvestro 19 Mon–Fri

9–6, Sat 9–2, Sun 9–8 ☎ 0800 160 000; **www.poste.it**
Other post offices Mon–Fri 8–1.30 or 2, Sat 8–1 (these times may vary slightly). Closed Sun.

ELECTRICITY

The power supply is 220 volts (125 volts in parts of Italy). Type of socket: round two- or three-hole sockets taking plugs of two round pins, or sometimes three pins in a vertical line. British visitors should bring an adaptor, US visitors will need a voltage transformer.

CURRENCY

The euro (€) is the official currency of Italy, which is divided into 100 cents. Coins come in denominations of 1, 2, 5, 10, 20 and 50 cents, €1 and €2, and notes come in €5, €10, €20, €50, €100, €200 and €500 denominations (the last two are rarely seen). The notes and one side of the coins are the same throughout the European single currency zone, but each country has a different design on one face of each of the coins. Notes and coins from any of the other countries can be used in Italy.

HEALTH AND SAFETY

Sun advice In summer, particularly in July and August, it can get oppressively hot and humid in cities. If 'doing the sights', cover up and apply a sunscreen (or dive into the shade of a museum), and drink plenty of fluids.

Drugs A pharmacy *(farmacia)*, recognized by a green cross sign, will employ highly trained staff able to offer medical advice on minor ailments and provide a wide range of prescription and non-prescription medicines and drugs. They take turns staying open through the afternoons and into late evening.

Safe water In some rural areas it is not advisable to drink the tap water *('acqua non potabile'* means 'the water is unsafe to drink'). However, across most of the rest of the

TIPS/GRATUITIES

Yes ✓ No ✗		
Restaurants (if service not included)	✓	10–15%
Cafés/bars	✓	€1 min
Taxis	✓	15%
Porters	✓	€1
Chambermaids	✓	€2 weekly
Cloakroom attendants	✓	€1
Hairdressers	✓	€2
Theatre/cinema usherettes	✗	
Toilets	✓	€1 min

country the water is perfectly safe, although most Italians prefer to drink bottled mineral water.

Safety Particularly in busy towns and tourist spots, petty theft is the main problem. The *carabinieri*, to whom thefts should be reported, wear black uniforms with red stripes down the outer seams of the trousers. Some precautions:

● Carry shoulder bags and cameras slung across your body.

● Scooter-borne bag-snatchers can be foiled if you keep on the inside of the pavement.

● Do not put anything down on a café or restaurant table.

● Lock car doors and never keep valuables in your car.

Carabinieri assistance:
☎ 112 from any call box

PHOTOGRAPHY

In general the light in Italy is good, although on sunny days there can be a bit of glare (particularly in the south) and in the north the light can be hazy. Most museums and certain churches will not allow you to photograph inside; check first.

Film and developing: A roll of film is called a *pellicola*, but 'film' should get you understood. Film and developing are more expensive in Italy than in the UK or USA.

CLOTHING SIZES

France	UK	Rest of Europe	USA	
46	36	46	36	
48	38	48	38	
50	40	50	40	
52	42	52	42	
54	44	54	44	Suits
56	46	56	46	
41	7	41	8	
42	7.5	42	8.5	
43	8.5	43	9.5	
44	9.5	44	10.5	
45	10.5	45	11.5	Shoes
46	11	46	12	
37	14.5	37	14.5	
38	15	38	15	
39/40	15.5	39/40	15.5	
41	16	41	16	
42	16.5	42	16.5	Shirts
43	17	43	17	
36	8	34	6	
38	10	36	8	
40	12	38	10	
42	14	40	12	
44	16	42	14	Dresses
46	18	44	16	
38	4.5	38	6	
38	5	38	6.5	
39	5.5	39	7	
39	6	39	7.5	
40	6.5	40	8	Shoes
41	7	41	8.5	

Best places to see

1 Basilica di San Pietro and Il Vaticano, Rome

www.vatican.va/museums

One of the world's biggest churches half fills one of its smallest states – the Vatican, headquarters of the Roman Catholic church and home to a vast museum.

The first **St Peter's** was built by Emperor Constantine over the saint's tomb, which is in the crypt. Today's awesome building was commissioned in 1503 by Pope Julius II, who appointed Bramante as the architect. Work lasted for more than 120 years and many people were involved: Michelangelo designed the dome, Carlo Maderno the façade, and Bernini the impressive colonnade.

Inside, on the right, is Michelangelo's *Pietà* of 1499. Other gems include a 13th-century bronze statue of St Peter, Bernini's Baldacchino and his monuments to popes Urban VIII and Alexander VII, and Giotto's mosaic of an angel. The spectacular view from the roof is framed by massive statues of Christ, John the Baptist and the Apostles (minus St Peter).

Behind the basilica lie the **Vatican museums** – too much for one visit, but several timed routes cover a selection of the highlights, including the Museo Gregoriano-Egizio Egyptian collection; the Museo Chiaramonti collection of Roman sculpture;

the Museo Pio Clementino, whose ancient art includes the Belvedere Apollo and Laocoön; the Museo Gregoriano–Etrusco's Greek, Roman and Etruscan art; and corridors of tapestries and 16th-century maps that lead to the four Raphael rooms. In the first is the famous School of Athens in which many of Raphael's contemporaries are portrayed as Greek philosophers and poets. The other rooms show biblical and early Christian scenes.

Next comes the Sistine Chapel. Michelangelo painted the ceiling between 1508 and 1512. The ceiling tells the story of the Creation, in which God is dividing light from darkness and water from land before creating the sun, the moon, Adam and Eve. The last four panels show the birth of original sin and the story of Noah. On the chapel's end wall is Michelangelo's much later *Last Judgement*.

Beyond the chapel are the Vatican library, a gallery of modern religious art, and collections of pagan and early Christian antiquities. The Pinacoteca (picture gallery) has a marvellous collection of medieval, Renaissance and baroque paintings, with masterpieces by most of the famous names in European art.

✚ 138 C1 🚇 Ottaviano 🚌 To Piazza del Risorgimento
ℹ Vatican Tourist Office ☎ 06 6988 4466

Basilica di San Pietro

🕓 Apr–Sep daily 7–7; Oct–Mar daily 7–6 ✋ Basilica: free; roof: moderate

Musei Vaticani

🕓 Mar–Oct Mon–Fri 8.45–4.45, Sat 8.45–1.45; Nov–Mar Mon–Sat 8.45–1.45; last Sun of month 9–1 (free)
✋ Expensive 🍴 Cafeteria (€)

2 Canal Grande, Venice

Dissecting the city, the Canal Grande is Venice's main thoroughfare, a magnificent, sinuous waterway lined with a procession of glorious buildings and *palazzi* that is unique in the world.

Running northwest to southeast, the Canal Grande is almost 4km (2.5 miles) long and varies in width from 30–70m (100–230ft), with an average depth of around 5m (16ft). Three *sestiere* (city wards), Cannaregio, San Marco and Castello, lie to the east

and three, San Polo, Santa Croce and Dorsoduro, to the west. The Canal is spanned by three bridges and served by seven *traghetti* stations, from where gondolas ply back and forth across its width. Lining its banks is an uninterrupted sequence of *palazzi* and churches, their main façades overlooking the water. Built over a period of more than four centuries, these superlative buildings stylistically cover the whole span of Venetian architecture, their combination of water, stone and light one of the world's truly great visual experiences.

The best, and indeed only, way to see everything is to take the No 1 *vaporetto* from the station to San Marco. Along the way, the main sights to look for include the Renaissance Palazzo Vendramin Calergi, winter home to the Casino (left), Longhena's 1652 Ca' Pesaro (right) and the beautiful Gothic Ca' d'Oro (left). Below this lies the Rialto, with its graceful bridge and vibrant markets, followed by a string of stately palaces, which includes the huge Ca' Foscari and the Ca' Rezzonico (right). Another bridge, the Accademia, brings you to the lower stretch, with the lagoon opening up, the plague church of the Salute to your right and the glories of San Marco ahead.

➕ 133 C7 (Venezia) ✋ *Vaporetto* ticket: moderate. Included in some city tours 🍽 Wide choice 🚏 Start at Piazzale Roma; end at San Marco
ℹ Piazza San Marco, San Marco 71f ☎ 041 529 8711

3 Costiera Amalfitana

www.ravelloapts.org
www.amalfitouristoffice.it

South of Naples lies the Amalfi Coast, a stretch of spectacular coastline, where ragged, grey cliffs plunge into an unbelievably turquoise Mediterranean.

Despite being one of Italy's busiest holiday haunts, it is still possible, among the summer crowds that fill the white fishing-villages-turned resorts, to feel the romance that has inspired generations of artists and songwriters. Even slightly over-developed Sorrento, a centre for package tours on the western end of the Costiera, has its peaceful corners, with views over the Bay of Naples to the islands of Capri (➤ 120) and Ischia. Further east is the more chic and expensive resort of Positano, clinging to the cliffside.

North and a little inland from here is **Ravello,** arguably the most stunning of the Amalfitana towns. The sea views are particularly good from exotic Villa Rufolo. Wagner stayed here in 1880 and based the magic gardens in *Parsifal* on those of the villa. The gardens of the Villa Cimbrone are equally evocative. Ravello's 11th-century Cathedral of San Pantaleone was renovated in the 18th century, but the bronze doors by Barisano da Trani (1179) have survived along with other elements of the earlier building, including an ornate 13th-century pulpit.

Amalfi is the largest town and, until the 12th century, it was a major maritime power. Its most

eye-catching sight is the 9th-century Cathedral of Sant'Andrea – although the sumptuous façade is a 19th-century restoration of a 13th-century original. Alongside is the 13th-century Chiostro del Paradiso (Cloister of Paradise), where Amalfi's most illustrious citizens were laid to rest.

✚ 136 B3

Ravello

🛈 Piazza Duomo 10 ☎ 089 857 977

Amalfi

🛈 Corso delle Repubbliche Marinare 19 ☎ 089 871 107

4 Duomo, Milan

www.duomomilano.com

The massive yet delicate Gothic Milan Cathedral, towering above its own vast, open piazza, is dramatically surrounded by bustling, modern Milan.

Even allowing for the decades it usually took to complete a cathedral, the Duomo of Milan was a long time in the making. Work started in 1386 under Prince Gian Galeazzo Visconti, continued over the following centuries in the hands of a host of European craftsmen, and was finished in 1809 under the orders of Napoleon. A trip on to the roof, with its views over Milan to the Alps glimpsed through a forest of 135 spires and 2,244 statues,

makes the long centuries of toil seem worthwhile.

At 157m (515ft) long and 92m (301ft) wide, this is the third-largest church in Europe after St Peter's (➤ 22–23) and Seville Cathedral. The façade is a surprisingly harmonious mishmash of styles from Gothic, through Renaissance and baroque to neoclassical. Beyond the bas-relief bronze doors depicting scenes from the lives of the Virgin and St Ambrose (Milan's patron saint), as well as Milanese history, is a contrastingly bare interior with 52 columns, each 48m (157ft) high, and numerous tombs and memorials lit by glorious 15th- and 16th-century stained-glass windows. Look in particular for a 12th-century bronze candelabrum and the gruesome statue of the flayed St Bartholomew holding his skin. The repeated symbol of a snake swallowing a man was the local Visconti family crest. The crypt contains the usual church treasures, as well as traces of the original 4th-century baptistery.

In the Museo del Duomo (Cathedral Museum), at Piazza del Duomo 14, the history of the cathedral's construction is shown alongside historic artefacts.

✠ 132 C3 (Milano) ☎ 02 8646 3456. Museum: 02 860 358 🕐 Treasury, crypt and roof: mid-Nov to Feb daily 9–4.45; Mar to mid-Nov daily 9–5.45. Baptistery: Tue–Sun 9.45–12.45, 2.45–5.45. Museum: daily 10–1.15, 3–6 💰 Museum and roof: moderate; treasury and crypt: inexpensive 🍴 Cafeteria (€)

5 Foro Romano, Palatino and Colosseo, Rome

www.capitolium.org
www.comune.roma.it

These atmospheric ruins represent the social, political, religious and business heart of ancient Rome.

You are immersed in Rome's history as soon as you enter the **Forum.** Left of the entrance is the Basilica Aemilia with traces of coins fused into its floor from a fire in the 5th century. Next, along the Sacred Way, is the (rebuilt) 3rd-century Curia where the Senate met, and the rostrum where orations were made. Opposite the Curia are three beautiful columns from the Temple of Castor and Pollux. The round building is the Temple of Vesta – the vestal virgins lived in the villa behind it. Opposite are the three massive vaults of the 4th-century AD Basilica of Maxentius and Constantine. The Arch of Titus, near the exit, was erected in the 1st century AD to celebrate the Emperor's sack of Jerusalem.

On the **Palatine Hill** overlooking the Forum are the remains of the emperors' gigantic palaces and traces of 7th-century BC huts.

The **Colosseum** was built by Emperor Vespasian in the 1st century AD. Tiered seating for more than 55,000 spectators overlooked a central ring where gladiators, other combatants and wild animals (kept in underground passages) fought each other to the death. Mock sea battles could also be staged, thanks to an underground water supply which allowed the arena to be flooded. Changing public

taste and the fall of Rome forced the Colosseum into disuse in the mid-6th century.

Foro and Palatino

✠ 139 E6 ✉ Via dei Fori Imperiali ☎ 06 3996 7700 (recorded information) ⏰ Daily 9–7.30. Closed 1 Jan and 25 Dec ♨ Foro free; Palatino expensive (includes Colosseo)

Colosseo

✠ 139 E 7 ✉ Piazza del Colosseo ☎ 06 3996 7700 ⏰ Apr–Sep daily 9–7.30; Oct–Mar daily 9–5.30 ♨ Included in Palatino

⑥ Galleria degli Uffizi, Florence

www.firenzemusei.it

Generations of the powerful Medici family amassed this collection of 13th- to 18th-century paintings, which is among the finest in the world.

The Uffizi, designed by Giorgio Vasari in 1560, was originally intended to house the government offices *(uffici)* of Florence and became home to the Medici art collections in 1588. The art was bequeathed to the city in 1737 by Anna Maria Luisa, the last of the Medici dynasty. Inside, 45 galleries are filled with world-famous masterpieces, hung in roughly chronological order to give an opulent overview of the development of mainly Italian art.

Early highlights include Giotto's *Ognissanti Madonna* (1310), showing his – for its time – revolutionary naturalism and use of perspective. Contrast it with the flatter Gothic styles of Simone Martini, Cimabue and Duccio. Throughout the 15th century the representation of perspective developed as the Renaissance got under way. Look for this in Paolo Uccello's *Battle of San Romano* (1456), Piero della Francesca's imposing profiles of the *Duke and Duchess of Urbino* (1465–70) and Fra Filippo Lippi's *Virgin and Child*. The magnificent Botticelli collection includes the *Birth of Venus* (1485) and *Primavera*

(1478) and there are two Leonardo da Vinci works: an *Annunciation* (1472–75) and an unfinished *Adoration of the Magi* (1481).

Michelangelo's *Holy Family* (1456), with its contorted poses and sculpted, draped fabrics, is an early example of Mannerism. Highlights from this period include Raphael's *Madonna of the Goldfinch* (1506), Parmigianino's *Madonna of the Long Neck* (1534), Titian's sultry *Venus of Urbino* (1538) and works by Caravaggio. Among the non-Italian masters represented are Cranach, Dürer, Holbein, Rubens, Van Dyck, Goya and Rembrandt.

✚ 133 F6 (Firenze) ✉ Loggiata degli Uffizi 6 ☎ 055 238 8651 🕓 Tue–Sun 8.15–6.50 (reservations advised: 055 294 883). Closed Mon, 1 Jan, 1 May, 25 Dec 🖐 Expensive 🍴 Cafeteria (€) 🚌 3, 11, 15, 23

Piazza San Marco, Venice

Generations of Venetians and visitors have frequented the smart, porticoed cafés that flank this vast, paved square.

The northeast side of the square is dominated by the façade and domes of the **Basilica di San Marco,** built between the 10th and 12th centuries, and added to over 300 years. Above the main entrance are copies of four 3rd-century or older bronze horses, looted from Constantinople in 1204; the originals are inside. The atrium contains superb Romanesque and Byzantine carvings and mosaics and gives access to the interior, covered with glittering mosaics from the 12th to 17th centuries. Treasures, such as the 14th-century Pala d'Oro altar screen, reflect Venice's strong Byzantine links, while the superb tessellated floor highlights the building's age. There are fabulous views from the adjoining 99m-high (325ft) Campanile.

Next to the basilica is the Palazzo Ducale (Doges' Palace), residence of the doges of Venice since the 9th century; the present Gothic building is late 14th century. Inside are the imposing meeting rooms of the

élite groups who ran Venice's complex internal and foreign affairs, lined with wall and ceiling paintings, many by Tintoretto and Veronese. The torture chamber and a labyrinth of dank prison cells hints at the far from benign nature of some aspects of Venetian government. Suspects were brought into the prison via the famous Bridge of Sighs behind the *palazzo*.

The **Museo Correr** is at the opposite end of the piazza. It has a fine collection of artefacts from the Renaissance onwards.

✚ 133 C7 (Venezia) 🍴 Plenty of cafés (€€€)

Basilica di San Marco

☎ 041 522 5205 🕐 May–Sep Mon–Sat 9.45–5.30 (4.30 Oct–Apr), Sun 2–4 ✋ Free

Museo Correr

☎ 041 520 9070 🕐 May–Oct daily 9–7; Nov–Apr daily 9–4 ✋ Expensive

8 Pompei

www.pompeiisites.org

The remains of this busy ancient city, buried when Vesuvius erupted in AD79, give some poignant glimpses of daily life in the Roman Empire.

Pompei has been under excavation for more than 250 years and, although only a few buildings are open to the public, there is far too much to see in one day. It is best to buy a detailed guide and map, visit your priority sights, and then wander to absorb the remarkable atmosphere of this beautiful site. Many of the major artistic finds are on display in the Museo Archeologico Nazionale (National Archaeological Museum) in Naples (▶ 116).

Among the most interesting houses are patrician and middle-class villas with statues, mosaics and frescoes, many of them erotic and/or mystic and difficult to interpret. Try to see the Casa dei Vetii,

the Casa del Fauno, the Casa del Poeta Tragico with its 'beware of the dog' sign and, if it's open, the Casa dei Misteri. Shops include a bakery, a cramped brothel with graphic wall paintings of the services offered, and a laundry where you can follow the complicated washing procedures used by ancient Romans. There are also numerous bars and food shops, many with large clay storage pots embedded into their serving hatches.

Public buildings include the forum with its basilica and temples, two

theatres, Italy's oldest surviving amphitheatre (80BC), baths and two gyms.

Throughout Pompei the cobbled streets are heavily grooved by the passage of inumerable carts, and the walls are spattered with snatches of carefully executed graffiti. The most moving memorials of the disaster are the casts of bodies of the victims (believed to be about 10 per cent of the 25,000 population), eternally frozen in the positions in which they died.

✚ 136 B3 ✉ Piazza Esedra 5, Pompei ☎ 081 857 5347
🕐 Apr–Oct daily 8.30–7.30 (last admission 6); Nov–Mar daily 8.30–5 (last admission 3.30). Closed 1 Jan and 25 Dec
♿ Expensive 🍴 Cafeteria (€)

Ravenna's Mosaics

www.turismo.ra.it

Ravenna, once capital of the Roman Empire, boasts 5th- to 6th-century churches containing the world's most accomplished Byzantine mosaics.

While much of the rest of western Europe was in Dark Ages decline, Ravenna was enjoying prosperity as an important provincial centre and, from around AD402, as the western capital of the Roman Empire. The city converted to Christianity in the 2nd century and much of its wealth went into building churches and other religious sites. The mosaics contain some of the earliest versions of Christian images such as the baptism of Christ, the Virgin, saints, martyrs and apostles with their symbols, and the cross. The best are housed in five sites across the historic centre.

The 5th-century **Battistero (Baptistery) Neoniano** is believed to be Ravenna's oldest monument. The mosaics show the baptism of Christ and the 12 Apostles. The cruciform **Mausoleo (Mausoleum) di Galla Placidia** (started in AD430) may not contain the remains

of the strong-willed Galla, but it does have charming mosaics of stars and flowers on the vaults and a Good Shepherd on the west wall. The dome of the **Battistero degli Ariani** (late 5th century) shows another baptism of Christ.

The finest mosaics in Ravenna are in two churches. **Sant'Apollinare Nuovo** (AD519) contains processions of saints bearing gifts to the Virgin and scenes from the life of Christ, all with gold backgrounds. **San Vitale** (consecrated AD547) has richly coloured mosaics full of flowers and birds and depicting Christ the King, Old Testament scenes, and Empress Theodora and Emperor Justinian.

✚ 133 E7 🕐 Daily 9–7. Closed 1 Jan, 25 Dec
✋ Take advantage of one of the two multi-entrance ticket options
ℹ Via Salara 8/12 ☎ 0544 35404

Battistero Neoniano
✉ Via Battistero

Mausoleo di Galla Placidia
✉ Via Fiandrini

Battistero degli Ariani
✉ Via degli Ariani

Sant'Apollinare Nuovo
✉ Via di Roma

San Vitale
✉ Via Fiandrini

10 Valle dei Templi, Sicily

The most extensive ancient Greek remains outside Greece, these nine ruined temples were once part of the city of Akragas.

Akragas (now Agrigento) was founded in 582BC by settlers from Rhodes. For nearly 200 years it flourished, with a temple complex that rivalled that of Athens. In 406BC, it was attacked by the Carthaginians, who pillaged the temples. Destruction was continued by zealous 6th-century Christians and earthquakes.

Eight of the temples lie west to east along a ridge south of Agrigento. Little remains of the Tempio di Vulcano (430BC), but nearby is a group of shrines for sacrifices to the underground (chthonic) gods. The strikingly positioned three columns are part of the so-called Tempio dei Dioscuri (Castor and Pollux), a 19th-century assemblage of bits and pieces from several buildings. Further on is the unfinished Tempio di Giove (Olympian Zeus), started in 480BC. Eight erect columns belong to the Tempio di Ercole (Hercules), built in 520BC and probably the oldest survivor in the valley. The Tempio della Concordia (Concord, 430BC) is especially well preserved. The 450BC Tempio di Hera (Juno) is set dramatically on top of the ridge. South is the Tempio di Esculapio (Aesculepius, god of healing).

✚ 140 F2 (Agrigento) ✉ Via dei Templi, Agrigento; Via Sacra, Agrigento ☎ 0922 26191 🕑 Daily 8.30 to one hour before sunset 🎟 Inexpensive 🍴 Restaurant (€€€) 🚌 Bus from Agrigento
ℹ Via Cesare Battisti 15, Agrigento ☎ 0922 20454

Exploring

Italy was one of the first tourist destinations in the world, with aristocratic Britons heading there in droves during their Grand Tour of Europe.

The attraction has endured and grown to mammoth proportions, and there are many reasons to explore Italy: a wealth of ancient ruins and monuments, spectacular mountain scenery (and winter sports), the gorgeous Italian Lakes in the north, vibrant cities, shops full of chic fashions in Milan and Rome, some of the best museums and art galleries in the world, picturesque coastal villages and beaches, little hilltop towns of Tuscany, boat rides to romantic islands… The list goes on and on.

And then, of course, there's Italian cuisine and world-class wines, and a people who combine a passionate approach to living with a laid back attitude in their day-to-day lives. It's a compelling blend.

Northwest Italy

Here tiny, remote mountain villages clinging to the foothills of the Alps seem to belong to a different world from the sophisticated cities of Milan and Turin, the fashionable resorts of the Riviera and the Lakes, and the historic splendour of medieval and Renaissance towns such as Mantua and Cremona.

The majestic mountains, the seemingly endless plains and the picture-postcard coasts of northwest Italy provide winter and summer sports that include skiing, mountaineering, swimming and sailing, and vast areas of unspoiled natural charm.

Then there are fantastic art collections and historic monuments, excellent cuisine, and superb *alta moda* shopping. In spite of all this natural and historic beauty, the northwest is also where many of Italy's most important industries and businesses are based, making it among the richest and most productive areas of Europe.

Milano (Milan)

What Rome, Florence and Venice are to romantic, historic Italy, Milan is to stylish, modern Italy. This busy metropolis is Italy's second largest city and, while Rome is the political capital, Milan can claim to be the capital of business, finance and industry. For most visitors Milan means chic Italian fashion, stylish bars and restaurants, bustling streets filled with smartly dressed locals brandishing *telefonini*, and the chance of seeing opera in the world-famous Teatro alla Scala. However, there is even more to Milan, and the city also boasts some splendid art collections and monuments.

🔢 132 C3

ℹ️ Palazzo del Turismo, Via Marconi 1 ☎ 02 7252 4301; www.milanoinfotourist.com

CASTELLO SFORZESCO

Most of the castle dates from the 15th century, with some later additions. It was the seat of the Sforza family, the dukes of Milan, until the late 19th century when it

first housed the city's collections of art, applied arts, archaeology and coins. Among the highlights are Michelangelo's unfinished sculpture, the *Pietà Rondanini*, and pictures by Mantegna, Bellini and Tiepolo; the Museo degli Strumenti Musicali (Musical Instruments Museum); and a collection of 18th- and 19th-century costumes.

www.milanocastello.it

✉ Piazza Castello ☎ 02 8846 3743 🕐 Tue–Sun 9–5.30. Closed public hols 💷 Free Ⓜ Lanza

DUOMO

See pages 28–29.

GALLERIA D'ARTE MODERNA

This gallery of modern art was opened in 1984 in the Villa Reale and is expanding. The emphasis is on 20th-century Italian artists. Foreign artists are also well represented.

✉ Villa Reale, Via Palestro 16 ☎ 02 7600 2819 🕐 Tue–Sun 9.30–5.30. Closed public hols 💷 Free Ⓜ Palestro

GALLERIA VITTORIO EMANUELE II

This luxurious 19th-century shopping arcade is packed with sophisticated shops, bars and restaurants. Look for the zodiac floor mosaics and representations of Europe, America, Africa and Asia under the impressive, airy glass dome.

✉ Piazza del Duomo and Piazza della Scala 🚇 Duomo

PINACOTECA AMBROSIANA

The *palazzo* was built in 1609 to house Cardinal Federico Borromeo's art collection and 30,000-volume library. An immaculate restoration job (1990–97), costing 45 billion *lire* (well over €21.7 million), has returned it to its original splendour. The paintings from the 14th to 19th centuries include works by Caravaggio, Raphael, Tiepolo, Titian and Giorgone. Special exhibitions occasionally feature some of the library's major manuscripts, which include a 5th-century illustrated *Iliad*, an early edition of Dante's *Commedia Divina* and Leonardo's Atlantic Codex.

www.ambrosiana.it

✉ Piazza Pio XI 2 ☎ 02 806 921, 02 8069 2225 🕐 Tue–Sun 10–5.30. Closed public hols 💶 Expensive 🚇 Cordusio

PINACOTECA DI BRERA

Milan's most important art gallery is housed in a 17th-century *palazzo* which became the Accademia di Belle Arti in the 18th century. Unlike many other Italian collections, this one includes later artists, among them Modigliani, Morandi, Picasso and Braque, as well as the 19th-century Italians, Francesco Hayez and Giovanni Fattori. But earlier periods are particularly well represented too, with masterpieces by Bramante, Caravaggio, Raphael, Canaletto, Van Dyck and Rubens; notable is Mantegna's *Dead Christ*, in which the artist makes disturbingly dramatic use of an unusual perspective.

✉ Via Brera 28 ☎ 02 722 631, 02 8942 1146 🕐 Tue–Sun 8.30–7.30 ✋ Moderate Ⓜ Lanza

SANTA MARIA DELLE GRAZIE

Bramante contributed to this attractive late 15th-century monastery by designing the dome, gallery and cloisters. The gem, however, is in the nearby refectory, where Leonardo da Vinci frescoed his much reproduced *Cenacolo (Last Supper)* on the north wall, between 1485 and 1497. Being a perfectionist, he never quite finished it; but more tragically, over the centuries the ravages of time, damp and warfare have taken their toll and the painting has deteriorated badly. It is nevertheless still spectacular.

✉ Piazza Santa Maria delle Grazie 2, Corso Magenta ☎ 02 8942 1146 🕐 Tue–Sun 8.15–7 ✋ Expensive Ⓜ Cadorna

What to See in Northwest Italy

AOSTA

The 'Rome of the Alps' is surrounded by stupendous mountains at the crossroads between the Mont Blanc and St Bernard tunnels. Although mainly used as a holidaymakers' stopover on the way to the Alps, it has an interesting centre with ancient Roman remains. These date back to the 1st century BC, when the city was founded as *Augusta Praetoria*, and include a theatre, an amphitheatre, a forum and the Arco di Augusto.

www.regione.vda.it/turismo

✚ 132 B1

🛈 Piazza Chanoux 2 ☎ 0165 236 627

CINQUE TERRE

One of the wildest stretches of the Ligurian coastline gets its name from five picturesque villages that cling to cliff edges and tumble down steep hillsides to pretty little bays. Although all the villages can be reached by train, only two of them are easily accessible by road – **Monterosso al Mare,** which is the largest of the Cinque Terre and has the biggest, busiest beaches, and Riomaggiore. Between lie Vernazza, founded by the Romans in a sheltered cove, and Corniglia and Manarola which have wonderful views of the sea. All are linked by steep footpaths.

www.cinqueterre.it

✚ 132 E4

Monterosso al Mare

🛈 Via Seggiano ☎ 0187 817 506

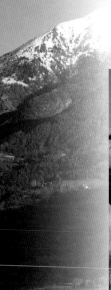

CREMONA

This is an important, agricultural market town with a strong musical tradition. As well as being the birthplace of composer Claudio Monteverdi (1567–1643), Cremona was where the first violins were made, in the 16th century, and where Antonio Stradivari (1644–1737), or 'Stradivarius' – the most famous violin-maker of all time – had his workshop. His drawings, models and violins can be seen in the **Museo Stradivariano.** The magnificent Romanesque-Gothic Duomo (1107–1332) is flanked by the 112m (367ft) Torrazzo tower, with its 15th-century astronomical clock.

www.aptcremona.it

➕ 132 D4

Museo Stradivariano

✉ Via Palestro 17 ☎ 0372 461 886 ◷ Tue–Sat 9–6, Sun and public hols 10–6. Closed 1 Jan, 1 May and 25 Dec 💷 Expensive

GENOVA (GENOA)

The birthplace of Christopher Columbus, Genoa has been an important maritime centre since the 11th century, and today its bustling, modern harbours form Italy's most important commercial port. The square 117m-high (383ft) lighthouse, called the *Lanterna* (renovated 1547), used to burn wood to guide ships into port, and the modern aquarium houses an exciting collection of marine life (plant and animal) in reconstructed natural habitats. Behind the Porto Vecchio is the **Duomo (San Lorenzo),** a mix of architectural styles from Romanesque to baroque, with a fine collection of relics in its Museo del Tesoro. Among the most interesting palaces in the city, the Palazzi Bianco and Rosso, on the Via Garibaldi, house important art collections, while the Palazzo del Principe gives an insight into how the aristocratic Doria family lived.

www.apt.genova.it

✚ 132 E3

Duomo San Lorenzo

✉ Piazza San Lorenzo ☎ 010 345 0048; Museo del Tesoro: 010 247 1831 🕓 Museo: Mon–Sat 9–11, 3–5.30 (guided tours only) 💵 Moderate

Aquarium

✉ Piazza Caricamento ☎ 010 234 5678; www.acquario.ge.it 🕓 Mar–Oct closed Tue; Nov–Feb closed Mon 💵 Expensive

LAGO MAGGIORE

This long, mountain-encircled lake runs up into Switzerland. Although some stretches of its banks are overdeveloped, other parts offer the most romantic of idealized lakeside scenery. The lake's most breathtaking features are the three Isole Borromee, owned by the Borromeo family. On Isola Bella, the 17th-century Carlo Borromeo III built a luxurious palace with spectacular gardens for his wife Isabella. Isola dei Pescatori has an attractive village on it, while Isola Madre is covered in gardens. On the lake's shores stand the attractive

towns of Angera, Baveno, Cannero Riviera and Verbania (its main centre), holiday destinations since Victorian times.

✚ 132 B3 🚢 Boats on the lake and to the islands from Verbania

Palazzo Borromeo

www.borromeoturismo.it

✉ Isola Bella ☎ 0323 30 556 ⏰ Apr–Oct daily 9–5.30 💷 Expensive

PAVIA

Throughout history, Pavia has been an important centre. As capital of the Lombard kings until 1359, it hosted the coronation of, among others, Charlemagne in 774. During the Middle Ages and the Renaissance its ancient 11th-century university could boast such alumni as Petrarch and Leonardo da Vinci. While the town itself is not short of impressive historic sights, Pavia's main draw lies a few kilometres north. The **Certosa di Pavia** (Charterhouse of Pavia) was founded in 1396 although most of the present buildings date from the 15th and 16th centuries. Behind a well-proportioned and exquisitely carved Renaissance façade, the interior is mainly Gothic, adorned with marquetry, frescoes and sculpture. In the first chapel on the left is an altarpiece by Perugino, flanked by works by Bergognone, who also painted frescoes in the transept. Some of the altars include semiprecious stones.

➕ 132 C3

Certosa di Pavia

✉ Viale del Monumento ☎ 0382 925 613 ⏰ May–Sep Tue–Sun 9–11.30, 2.30–5.30 (Oct–Apr closes at sunset) 💵 Donation 🚉 Certosa station

RIVIERA LIGURE

From Ventimiglia in the west to La Spezia in the east, with Genoa (▶ 52) in the middle, the Ligurian coast is known as the Riviera Ligure. The towns and resorts along this stretch cover a range of

styles and tastes from the fishing-village charm of the Cinque Terre (➤ 50), through historic Cervo, Albenga, Rapallo and Portovenere to the revamped 19th-century aristocratic exuberance of San Remo. Near the French border is the **Villa Hanbury,** with gardens of exotic plants first laid out by English botanist Sir Thomas Hanbury in the 1860s and 1870s. On a peninsula, east of Genoa, is the chic sailing resort of Portofino.

🚰 132 E3

Villa Hanbury

✉ Corso Monte Carlo 43, Località Mortola ☎ 0184 229 507 ⏱ Jun–Sep daily 9.30–6; Apr–May, Oct daily 10–5; Nov–Mar Thu–Tue 10–4 💶 Expensive

TORINO (TURIN)

Turin is the capital of the Italian motor industry. The Fabbrica
Italiana Automobili Torino (FIAT) was founded here in 1899 and
became one of the largest businesses in Europe. Today, having
expanded and bought several other Italian car manufacturers, it
accounts for nearly 80 per cent of the cars made in Italy.
Proprietors, the Agnelli family, also own Italy's most famous
football team, Juventus. Turin is also a city of art and, most
famously, home of the Turin Shroud. It is kept in the Cappella della
Sacra Sindone, next to the 15th-century **Duomo** and, although it is
rarely on display, it continues to attract the faithful. The nearby
Palazzo Reale, former residence of the Savoy royal family, contains
many artistic treasures. Other sights include the Palazzo
dell'Accademia delle Scienze, which houses the Galleria Sabauda
painting collection and the important Egyptian museum; the
façade of the Palazzo Carignano, united Italy's first parliament
building; and the elegant main shopping street, Via Roma.
www.turismotorino.org
➕ 132 C2 ✈ Aeroporto Caselle

Duomo
✉ Piazza San Giovanni ☎ 011 436 1540

Northeast Italy

Most people come to northeast Italy to see Venice, whose magnetic charm attracts about 12 million tourists every year. However, there are plenty of other things to see and do in this scenically varied area, which stretches from the majestic, rocky Dolomites to the seemingly unending flatness of the Po Valley.

For a start, its cuisine, particularly that of the Emilia-Romagna region, is renowned throughout Italy. Medieval prosperity, often based on trade with the East, has left a heritage of churches and imposing civic buildings. They complement the stately palaces, elegant villas and priceless art collections of the powerful families and prince-bishops who ruled the area throughout much of its history and attracted some of the greatest artistic and architectural geniuses of all time.

Venezia (Venice)

One of the most painted, filmed and written about cities in the world, Venice is disturbingly beautiful; nothing quite prepares you for that first glimpse of distant domes and spires emerging from the flat, grey waters like a mirage. Within the city, murky canal water laps the bases of dreamlike buildings, creating a slightly disorienting, rocking effect enhanced by the gentle rattle of the wind in boats and mooring poles.

✚ 133 C7

ℹ Piazza San Marco 71/F ☎ 041 529 8711; www.turismovenezia.it

ACCADEMIA, GALLERIA DELL'

This is the place to see Venetian art from the 14th to 18th centuries. While 14th-century artists (such as the Veneziano brothers) reflect the Byzantine and International Gothic movements that swept Europe, from the Renaissance onwards

Venetian artists (such as Giorgione, Lotto, Titian, Tintoretto and Veronese) developed a style that made greater use of colour and softer, more sensuous lines than their contemporaries elsewhere were using.

www.galleriaaccademia.org

✉ Campo della Carità ☎ 041 522 2247; advance reservations 041 520 0345

🕐 Tue–Sun 8.15–7.15, Mon 8.15–2. Closed 1 Jan, 1 May, 25 Dec

✋ Expensive

CA' D'ORO (GOLDEN HOUSE)

Regarded as the most beautiful *palazzo* in Venice, the lacy, Gothic façade of this stately residence (built 1420–34), used to be richly decorated with gold leaf and other luxurious materials. Now it houses the Galleria Giorgio Franchetti, the musician's spectacular collection of sculpture, tapestry and painting, which was donated to the state in 1916.

www.cadoro.org

✉ Calle Ca' d'Oro ☎ 041 523 8790

🕐 Tue–Sun 8.15–7.15, Mon 8.15–2. Closed 1 Jan, 1 May, 25 Dec ✋ Inexpensive

MADONNA DELL'ORTO

Inside this 15th-century Gothic church, tucked away in a corner of Cannaregio, are the tomb of the painter Tintoretto and some fine examples of his work. Most noteworthy of the paintings are a dramatic *Last Judgement* (to the right of the chancel) and an *Adoration of the Golden Calf*, on the left.

✉ Campo Madonna dell'Orto ☎ 041 719 933 🕐 Mon–Sat 10–5, Sun 1–5 ✋ Inexpensive

PIAZZA SAN MARCO
See pages 34–35.

SANTA MARIA GLORIOSA DEI FRARI
This sprawling Gothic church is packed with masterpieces by famous artists. Among them are a Donatello statue of John the Baptist (1450) to the right of the altar, a Bellini altarpiece in the sacristy, Titian's *Assumption of the Virgin* (1518) above the main altar, and Pietro Lombardo's carved rood-screen (1475). Among the many tombs and memorials are Canova's surprising pyramidical tomb (1822), based on one of his own designs, and a memorial to Titian.

✉ Campo dei Frari 🕐 Mon–Sat 9–6, Sun and public hols 1–6 ☎ 041 522 2637 ♿ Inexpensive

SANTI GIOVANNI E PAOLO
Also known as San Zanipolo, this severe 14th-century Dominican church made the perfect setting for the Doges' funerals. They were held here from 1450 and the church contains many of their tombs. Among the most interesting are those by Pietro Lombardo,

especially the arched tomb of Andrea Vendramin (1476–78), to the left of the altar. Other gems here include a magnificent polyptych by Bellini (1465), to the right of the entrance, and works by Veronese. The equestrian statue of Bartolomeo Colleoni (1480s) in the piazza outside is by Andrea Verrocchio.

✉ Campo Santi Giovanni e Paolo ☎ 041 523 5913 🕐 Mon–Sat 7.30–7, Sun 3–6 ✋ Inexpensive

SCUOLA GRANDE DI SAN ROCCO

Anyone with any interest in Tintoretto should visit this building, erected between 1515 and 1549 to house a charitable religious order. Its two floors contain more than 50 Tintoretto paintings executed from 1564 to 1587, including some of his greatest works, such as the sombre *Crucifixion* (1565) and eight scenes from the *Life of the Virgin* (1583–87). There are a few works by other artists, including Titian and the sculptor Francesco Pianta, whose caricature bust of Tintoretto in the upper hall is recognisable from the master's own self-portrait at the entrance to the Sala dell'Albergo.

www.scuolagrandesanrocco.it

✉ Campo San Rocco ☎ 041 523 4864 🕐 Apr–Oct daily 9–5.30; Nov–Mar daily 10–4. Closed 1 Jan, Easter, 25 Dec ✋ Expensive; free 16 Aug (Saint's Day)

What to See in Northeast Italy

BOLOGNA

The capital of Emilia-Romagna is a cultured, prosperous city of arcaded streets and historic monuments. It has one of the oldest universities in Europe (13th century or earlier), which numbers the inventor of radio, Guglielmo Marconi, among its alumni. In the heart of Bologna is the Piazza del Nettuno, with a magnificent Neptune fountain (1566) sculpted by Giambologna. The Basilica di San Petronio (started in 1390) has a spacious, calm interior with

high, vaulted ceilings and exquisite biblical bas-relief doors (1425–38) by Jacopo della Quercia. Opposite is the Renaissance Palazzo del Podestà. To the east are two 12th-century *torri pendenti* (leaning towers), survivors of the nearly 200 towers built in the Middle Ages by local nobles.

The nearby church of **San Giacomo Maggiore** contains the magnificent chapel of the Bentivoglio family, with frescoes, paintings and della Quercia's Bentivoglio tomb (1435). The **Pinacoteca Nazionale** has in its important collection works by Bolognese painters Guido Reni, Guercino and the Carracci. Also worth a visit is the **Abbazia di Santo Stefano,** a complex of four medieval churches dating for the most part from the 11th century.

✚ 133 E6 ✖ Aeroporto Marconi

San Giacomo Maggiore

✉ Piazza Rossini ☎ 051 225 970 🕓 Apr–Oct daily 10–1, 3–7; Nov–Mar daily 10–1, 2–8 💷 Donation

Pinacoteca Nazionale

✉ Via delle Belle Arti 56 ☎ 051 243 222; www.pinacotecabologna.it 🕓 Tue–Sun 9–6.30. Closed Mon and public hols 💷 Moderate

Abbazia di Santo Stefano

✉ Via Santo Stefano ☎ 051 223 256 🕓 Mon–Sat 9–12, 3.30–6; Sun and public hols 9–1, 3.30–6.30

BRESSANONE

Known as Brixen by its German-speaking population, this delightful medieval Alpine town lies on the road to Austria. Until 1803 it was ruled by a prince-bishop, whose sumptuous palace (rebuilt in 1595 over a 14th-century original) now houses a museum of art and local history. The 18th-century Duomo has a beautiful 13th-century cloister with 15th-century frescoes.

www.brixen.org

✚ 133 A6

ℹ Via Stazione 9 ☎ 0472 836 401

DOLOMITI (DOLOMITES)

Right up in the north of Italy, nestling under Austria, is the German-speaking Alto Adige (or Südtirol), much of it covered by the Dolomite mountains, which look as though they've been carved, folded and squeezed into an extraordinary variety of gnarled crags. Although this is Italy, the language, scenery, architecture and much of the culture are strongly influenced by Austria, and nearly all the place names have versions in German. The capital of Alto Adige is Bolzano (or Bozen), which has a fine 15th-century Gothic Duomo, and the **Museo Archeologico dell'Alto Adige,** whose highlight is the 5,300-year-old mummified corpse of what was probably a murder victim. To the west of this is a string of mountain resorts from which cable-cars carry skiers in winter, hillwalkers in summer and view-seekers all year round up into the mountains.

www.bolzano-bozen.it

🚩 133 B6 🚌 To Bolzano, then buses to other centres

Museo Archeologico dell'Alto Adige

✉ Via Museo 43 ☎ 0471 982 098; www.iceman.it ⏰ Tue–Sun 10–6 (Thu 10–8). Closed 1 Jan, 1 May, 25 Dec ✋ Expensive

FERRARA

This evocative old walled town, ruled by the rich and powerful Este family for centuries, is slightly off the beaten tourist track. The historic centre, with its Renaissance grid layout, contains some marvellous buildings. Chief among these are a 12th-century Duomo with a spectacular arched façade showing scenes from the Last Judgement, and **Castello Estense** (started 1385), the fairytale moated seat of the Este family, whose rivals were left to rot in its chilling dungeons. Among the most beautiful *palazzi* are Palazzo Schifanoia, another Este residence, started in 1385 and with murals by local painters, and **Palazzo dei Diamanti,** now an art gallery and museum. In winter, dense white mists rise up from the nearby River Po and smother the entire area.

✚ 133 D6

ℹ Castello Estense ☎ 0532 209 370

Castello Estense

✉ Largo Castello 🕐 Tue–Sun 9.30–5. Closed 25 Dec ✋ Moderate

Palazzo dei Diamanti

✉ Piazza Comunale ☎ 0532 205 844 🕐 Tue, Wed, Fri 9–2, Sat 9–7, Sun 9–1 ✋ Moderate

MANTOVA (MANTUA)

Set in the featureless expanse of the Lombard plain, the beautiful city of Mantua, surrounded on three sides by water, is approached through dreary 20th-century suburbs. Persevere, and you'll find yourself in a wonderfully preserved city, which, under the rule of the Gonzaga family, was home to one of Europe's most glittering Renaissance courts. Three lovely, interlocking squares lie at its heart, one of which is home to the **Palazzo Ducale,** seat of the Gonzagas, whose frescoed portraits by local painter Mantegna (1431–1505) can be seen in the Camera degli Sposi. The same family's **Palazzo del Tè** was designed and sumptuously decorated by Giulio Romano in 1525–35. Romano was also responsible for the stuccoes inside the Duomo, while the façade of the Basilica di Sant'Andrea is the work of the pioneer Renaissance architect Alberti (1404–72).

✚ 133 C5

Palazzo Ducale

✉ Piazza Sordello 40 ☎ 0376 382 150 🕐 Tue–Sun 9–6.30. Closed 1 Jan, 1 May, 25 Dec ✋ Expensive

Palazzo del Tè

✉ Viale Tè ☎ 0376 323 266 🕐 Tue–Sun 9–6 ✋ Expensive

MODENA

Founded as the Roman colony of Mutina, Modena has flourished throughout much of its history and is now associated with those symbols of modern prosperity, Ferrari and Maserati cars, which are manufactured in its outskirts. Among the principal sights of its winding medieval streets and pretty piazzas is a particularly fine Romanesque Duomo (started in 1099), with an 88m-high (288ft) Gothic tower, La Ghirlandina. On its west façade are 12th-century reliefs by Wiligelmo; inside, the rood-screen has scenes from the Passion. Within the **Palazzo dei Musei** is the massive Este Biblioteca (library) of rare, historic manuscripts and the family's collection of works by mainly local artists.

✚ 133 D5

Palazzo dei Musei

✉ Largo di Porta Sant'Agostino 337 ☎ Galleria: 059 439 5711; Biblioteca: 059 222 248 ◷ Galleria: Tue–Sun 8.30–7; Biblioteca: Mon–Thu 8.30–7, Fri 8.30–3.30, Sat 8.30–1. Closed public hols 💷 Moderate

PADOVA (PADUA)

This stately old university town has a matchless collection of historic and artistic treasures. At the top of the list is the **Cappella degli Scrovegni,** a 14th-century building adorned with Giotto's elegant, soothing frescoes of scenes from the Life of Christ. Reopened in March 2002 after extensive restoration, visitors now have to make reservations in advance (▶ 67). Around the altar of the 13th-century Basilica di Sant'Antonio are Donatello's bronze reliefs of the saint's life (1444). The Donatello statue of the *condottiere* (mercenary soldier) Gattamelata, outside, was the first equestrian statue of the Renaissance. Other gems include the

Chiesa and Museo degli Eremitani, both packed with priceless Renaissance art and historic artefacts, including two frescoes by Mantegna, the only ones to survive a bombing raid in 1944; the 16th-century anatomy theatre in the University's Palazzo del Bo; Titian's first known works in the Scuola del Santo; and the 16th-century Duomo, designed in part by Michelangelo.

www.padovanet.it; www.turismopadova.it

✚ 133 C6

Cappella degli Scrovegni

✉ Piazza Ermitani ☎ 049 201 0020 ⏰ Daily 9–7. Book at least 24 hours in advance on 049 202 0020. Closed public hols 🖑 Expensive

PARMA

Not only is Parma one of the eating capitals of Italy, but it also has some fine buildings and works of art. The main cupola of the Romanesque Duomo is covered with Correggio's *Assumption* (1534), while in the south transept is a 12th-century frieze showing the Descent from the Cross. Perpendicular to the Duomo is an exquisite 16-sided baptistery (1196, by Benedetto Antelami), with unrivalled 13th-century reliefs and frescoes depicting the Life of Christ. The **Galleria Nazionale** has a fine collection of 14th- to 18th-century art.

www.turismo.comune.parma.it

✚ 133 D5

Galleria Nazionale

✉ Piazzale della Pilotta 15 ☎ 0521 233 309 ⏰ Tue–Sun 9–2. Closed 1 Jan, 1 May, 25 Dec 🖑 Expensive

RAVENNA

See pages 38–39.

RIMINI

Rimini's vibrant seafront hides an interesting and attractive historic centre which is based around Piazza Cavour and the 14th-century Palazzo del Podestà. The most important monument is the church, the Tempio Malestiano, designed in 1450 by Renaissance architect Leon Battista Alberti, with frescoes by Piero della Francesca.

www.riminiturismo.it

✚ 133 E7

TRENTO

This attractive town is surrounded by mountains. Its Romanesque-Gothic Duomo was where the Council's decrees were proclaimed. Piazza del Duomo contains the medieval Palazzo Pretorio and some 16th-century frescoed houses. The magnificent **Castello del Buonconsiglio** has frescoes by Romanino and others, and houses part of the province's art collection.

✚ 133 B6

Castello del Buonconsiglio

✉ Via Bernardo Clesio 5 ☎ 0461 233 770 ◷ Apr–Sep Tue–Sun 10–5.30; Oct–Mar Tue–Sun 9–12, 2–5. Closed 1 Jan, 1 May, 25 Dec 👋 Moderate

TREVISO

Treviso's walled centre is full of meandering streets and graceful canals. The medieval and Renaissance buildings of Piazza dei Signori include the church of Santa Lucia, with frescoes by Tommaso da Modena (14th century). Gothic San Nicolò contains more da Modena frescoes, as well as works by Lorenzo Lotto and others, while the 15th- to 16th-century Duomo has a Titian altarpiece and an 11th-century baptistery. There is good Renaissance art in the **Museo Civico.**

✚ 133 C7

Museo Civico

✉ Borgo Cavour 24 ☎ 0422 658442 ◷ Tue–Sat 9–12.30, 2.30–5, Sun 9–12. Closed public hols 👋 Inexpensive

TRIESTE

Trieste is built on the sea, with most of its hinterland in Slovenia.
It has a long maritime tradition and among its places of interest are
the Museo del Mare, which traces the history of seafaring. In the
town centre is the fascinating Duomo San Giusto, a 14th-century
building linking two 5th-century basilicas that contains spectacular
12th-century mosaics. The splendid 15th- to 16th-century **Castello
di San Giusto,** with wonderful views, houses a museum with a
good weapons and armour collection.

www.triestetourism.it

✚ 133 C8

Castello di San Giusto

✉ Piazza Cattedrale 3 ☎ 040 313 636 or 040 309 362 ☀ Apr–Sep daily 9–7;
Oct–Mar daily 9–5. Closed public hols ✋ Inexpensive

UDINE

This pretty, hilly town has excellent views over Friuli towards the Alps from the 16th-century Castello. The Piazza della Libertà contains the Porticato di San Giovanni with its 1527 clocktower. The nearby Arco Bollani was designed by Palladio (1556). The artist Giambattista Tiepolo (1696–1770) was very active in Udine and his works grace the **Palazzo Arcivescovile** (Archbishop's Palace), the Musei Civici and the 14th-century Duomo.

🕇 133 B8

Palazzo Arcivescovile

✉ Piazza Patriarcato ☎ 0432 25 003 🕐 Wed–Sun 10–2, 3.30–6.30
✋ Moderate

VERONA

Verona attracts plenty of tourists to its 1st-century BC Roman theatre for outdoor opera in summer. Among its other important monuments is the ornate Romanesque church of **San Zeno Maggiore** (1123–35). Bronze door panels (11th and 12th century) depict scenes from the Bible and the life of San Zeno, while the interior's highlights include a ship's keel ceiling (1376) and an altarpiece by Mantegna (1450s). The two main squares are the Piazza dei Signori, with the 12th-century Palazzo del Comune (town hall) among its medieval and Renaissance civic gems, and the Piazza delle Erbe, with a busy market. The Scaligeri family, who governed the town from 1260 to 1387, are commemorated by a 14th-century bridge leading to the **Castelvecchio,** and by the Arche Scaligere, their opulent tombs.

www.tourism.verona.it

🕇 133 C5

San Zeno Maggiore

✉ Piazza San Zeno 🕐 Mon–Sat 8.30–6, Sun 1–6. Closed during services

Castelvecchio

✉ Corso Castelvecchio 2 ☎ 045 806 2611 🕐 Tue–Sun 8.30–7.30, Mon 1.30–7.30. Closed public hols ✋ Moderate

VICENZA

This genteel, gracious city is rich in the works of its most illustrious son, the architect Andrea Palladio (1508–80). Most famous of these is the villa **La Rotonda,** outside the city, which has been copied all over the world. His first public commission was the double-colonnaded Basilica in Piazza dei Signori, where he also designed the Loggia del Capitaniato. Among his other buildings are the Teatro Olimpico (1579), the oldest covered theatre in Europe, and many of the *palazzi* on the Corso Andrea Palladio. The Museo Civico (in another Palladio building) has splendid Gothic and Renaissance art, while older monuments include the Gothic churches of Santa Corona and San Lorenzo and some of the buildings on Contrà Porti, untouched by Palladio.

www.ascom.vi.it

✚ 133 C6

🛈 Piazza Matteotti 12 ☎ 0444 320 854

La Rotonda

✉ Via Rotonda 29 (about 2km/1.2 miles from Vicenza) ☎ 0444 321 793

🕐 Mid-Mar to Oct: gardens Tue–Sun 10–12, 3–6; interior Wed 10–12, 3–6. Nov to mid-Mar: gardens Tue–Sun 10–12, 2.30–5 💷 Expensive

Tuscany and Northern Central Italy

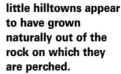

Populated by the highly cultured Etruscans centuries before the Romans rose to power, this is an area where rural and urban beauty blend harmoniously. While the landscape seems almost to have been sculpted by the Renaissance artists whose works are everywhere, the little hilltowns appear to have grown naturally out of the rock on which they are perched.

Travellers have been flocking to central Italy for centuries to enjoy the way of life that comes with a pleasant climate, excellent food and wines and an unequalled quantity and quality of art and architecture. For many this is quintessential Italy and, although you will have to share its spectacular sights with many others, the quiet confidence that comes from a long and prosperous history imbues even the busiest piazza with a soothing calm and a sense of continuity.

Firenze (Florence)

Florence is Renaissance Italy at its civilized best. The most accomplished artists and architects of the period flocked to Florence from all over central Italy to work for the powerful families. Today, the compact historic centre of Tuscany's busy capital is a mass of masterpieces from that flourishing era.

✚ 133 F6

ℹ Via Cavour 1 ☎ 055 290 832; www.firenzeturismo.it; www.firenze.net

DUOMO AND BATTISTERO

The Duomo's lavish exterior includes Giotto's 85m-high (278ft) campanile (1334) and reliefs by Pisano and Lucca della Robbia.

The massive dome (1465), by Brunelleschi, was the largest of its time. The façade is 19th-century. Inside are intricate marble inlaid floors (16th-century), Vasari frescoes in the dome, and works by Lucca della Robbia, Ghiberti, Uccello and others. There's more art in the Museo dell'Opera del Duomo (Mon–Sat 9–7.30, Sun 9–1.40). The nearby baptistery has splendid carved doors by Ghiberti and Pisano (Mon–Sat 12–7, Sun 8.30–2).

✉ Piazza del Duomo ☎ 055 230 2885

🕐 Duomo: Mon–Wed, Fri 10–5, Thu 10–3.30, Sat 10–4.45, Sun 1.30–4.45; Campanile and Dome: Mon–Fri 9–7, Sat 10–4.45; (last entry 45 mins before closing). Reduced hours first Sat of each month. Closed religious hols

✋ Duomo: free; Campanile and Dome: moderate 🚌 1, 11, 17, 23a

GALLERIA DELL'ACCADEMIA

Modern Europe's first art school, the Accademia delle Belle Arti, was founded here in 1563, and many of its original exhibits were acquired for the students to study and copy. Today the main pull of this collection of 15th- to 19th-century Tuscan art is the Michelangelo sculpture, including the (surprisingly enormous) original of his seductive *David* (1504), created for Piazza della Signoria (▶ 78), where a copy now stands. Among the other outstanding exhibits here are the four bound *Slaves or Prisoners* (unfinished, 1521–23) by Michelangelo, meant for the tomb of Pope Julius II.

✉ Via Ricasoli 60 ☎ 055 238 8612 🕐 Tue–Sun 8.30–6.20. Closed public hols ✋ Expensive 🚌 Many routes

GALLERIA DEGLI UFFIZI

See pages 32–33.

MUSEO NAZIONALE DEL BARGELLO

This imposing *palazzo* (1255–1345) was the city governor's residence, then from 1574 the police headquarters; public executions were held in its courtyard until 1786. It became one of Italy's first national museums in 1865. What the Uffizi (➤ 32–33) is to Renaissance painting, the Bargello is to sculpture – many of its exhibits came from the same Medici collections. Michelangelo's works include his first freestanding sculpture, *Bacchus* (1497), while other highlights are Donatello's jaunty *David* (1430), bas-reliefs (1402) by Brunelleschi and Lorenzo Ghiberti, and bronzes by Benvenuto Cellini (1500–71).

⊠ Via del Proconsolo 4 ☎ 055 238 8606 🕒 Tue–Sat, 2nd and 4th Sun of month and 1st, 3rd and 5th Mon of month 8.15–1.50. Closed public hols
✋ Moderate 🚌 19

PALAZZO MEDICI-RICCARDI

Generally acclaimed as the finest example of Florentine Renaissance architecture, the *palazzo* was started in 1444 by Michelozzo for Cosimo Medici the Elder and was the family's home until 1540. Michelangelo may have designed the windows (1517) next to the entrance. In the elegant courtyard are sculptures, and on one of the upper floors is the Cappella dei Magi with frescoes (1459) by Benozzo Gozzoli.

✉ Via Cavour 3 ☎ 055 276 0340. Advance reservations: 055 294 883
🕐 Thu–Tue 9–7. Closed Wed, public hols ♿ Moderate 🚌 1, 6, 7, 11, 12, 14

PALAZZO PITTI AND GIARDINO DI BOBOLI

Possibly designed by Brunelleschi (1458) for the Pitti banking family, this grandiose *palazzo* was their ostentatious attempt to outdo the Medici who, however, were to buy it from the declining Pitti in 1550. It now houses several museums, the most important of which is the Galleria Palatina, where a rich collection of Renaissance masterpieces is hung in frescoed halls. When open, the 17th-century state apartments are well worth seeing, as are the Galleria del Costume's clothes from the 18th to 20th centuries. Next to the *palazzo* are the Boboli Gardens. Laid out for the Medici after 1550, they are a splendid example of 16th- and 17th-century garden design, with much use of water, statues and formal layouts.

✉ Piazza Pitti ☎ 055 238 8614 🕐 Palace: Tue–Sun 8.15–6.50. Gardens: Jun–Aug, 8–6.30; Nov–Feb, 8–4.30; Mar and Sep, 8–6.30; Oct 8–5.30 (closed first and last Mon of month). Closed public hols ♿ Palace expensive, gardens moderate 🚌 15, 32, 37, 42

PIAZZA DELLA SIGNORIA

The political and social heart of Florence is an outdoor art gallery with Ammanati's Fontana di Nettuno (1575) and a copy of Michelangelo's *David* (now in the Galleria dell'Accademia, ➤ 75) among the works that stand outside the Loggia dei Lanzi (1382). In the Loggia are Roman statues, Cellini's *Perseus* (1554) and Giambologna's powerful *Rape of the Sabine Women* (1583). The piazza is dominated by the **Palazzo Vecchio** (1332), a monument to civic worthiness puffed out beneath its 94m (308ft) tower. Its imposing rooms are packed with art by Michelangelo, Vasari, Bronzino, Domenico Ghirlandaio and others.

Palazzo Vecchio

✉ Piazza della Signoria ☎ 055 276 8465 🕐 Mon–Wed, Fri–Sun 9–7, Thu 9–2 (summer Mon and Fri 9–11pm). Closed public hols ✋ Moderate (includes admission to Santa Maria del Carmine ➤ 80) 🚌 9, 23, 31, 32

PONTE VECCHIO

Florence's oldest and most charming bridge, with little shops and houses clinging precariously to the sides, was designed by Taddeo Gaddi (Giotto's pupil) in 1345.

✉ Lungarno Archibuscieri 🚌 Many routes

SAN LORENZO

The bare, unfinished façade of this Brunelleschi church (1442–46) hides a Renaissance treasure trove. The bronze pulpits are Donatello's (finished by his pupils in 1460), as are the sacristy decorations and doors (1435–43); the staircase, desks and ceiling of the Biblioteca Medicea Laurenziana are by Michelangelo; and a Bronzino fresco (1659) and some spectacular Medici monuments adorn the church.

✉ Piazza di San Lorenzo ☎ 055 216 634 🕐 Mon–Sat 10–5; closed Sun and public hols; Biblioteca: Mon–Sat 8.30–1.30 💲 Biblioteca: free; Church: inexpensive 🚌 Many routes

SAN MARCO

Founded in the 13th century, the convent of San Marco was extended by Michelozzo in 1437. Some cells and parts of the building are decorated with frescoes by Fra Angelico (1430s and 1440s), including a

hauntingly lovely *Annunciation*. These form part of the Museo di San Marco, along with a collection of other Renaissance masterpieces.

✉ Piazza di San Marco ☎ 055 238 8608 🕐 Mon–Fri 8.15–1.50; alternate Sat and Sun in month 8.15–7. Closed 1 Jan, 1 May, 25 Dec 💲 Expensive 🚌 Many routes

SANTA CROCE

The spacious interior of this Franciscan church (1294 onwards) holds the tombs of Michelangelo (1570, by Vasari), Machiavelli and other Renaissance greats. The artworks are too numerous to mention, but include Luca della Robbia roundels in Brunelleschi's Cappella dei Pazzi, Giotto frescoes in the Cappelle Bardi and Peruzzi, a Donatello wooden crucifix, and frescoes (including an early night scene) by Taddeo Gaddi.

✉ Piazza di Santa Croce ☎ 055 244 619 ⏰ Mon–Sat 9.30–5.30, Sun 1–5.30 ✋ Moderate (includes church and museum) 🚌 11, 19, 31, 32

SANTA MARIA DEL CARMINE

Fortunately the magnificent Cappella Brancacci frescoes survived a fire which badly damaged the rest of the church in the 18th century. The frescoes, depicting the Life of St Peter, were started by Masolino (1420s) and finished by Filippino Lippi (1480), but the bulk of them are by Masolino's pupil, the Renaissance pioneer Masaccio (1401–28). His realism, expressiveness and use of perspective were carefully studied by subsequent artists. Look for the anguished *Adam and Eve Being Expelled from Eden* (to the left of the chapel), and the facial expressions of characters in the other scenes.

✉ Piazza del Carmine ☎ 055 238 2195 ⏰ Mon, Wed–Sat 10–5, Sun 1–5. Closed public hols, 7 Jan, 16 Jul ✋ Moderate (includes admission to Palazzo Vecchio ➤ 78) 🚌 15

SANTA MARIA NOVELLA

Three founders of the Renaissance movement are represented in this beautiful 13th-century church, with its outstanding stained-glass windows: Alberti, with his dramatic black-and-white marble façade (1458); Brunelleschi, with his wooden crucifix; and Masaccio, whose use of perspective in the splendid *Trinity* fresco (1428) was revolutionary for its time. In addition, there are frescoes (1485) by Domenico Ghirlandaio in the Cappella Tornabuoni, while the museum housed in the church's cloisters contains numerous important frescoes, including some by Uccello. These were badly damaged in 1966 when the River Arno flooded.

✉ Piazza di Santa Maria Novella ☎ 055 215 918 🕐 Church: Mon–Thu and Sat 9.30–4.30, Fri and Sun 1–4.30; Museum: Mon–Sat 9–4.30, Sun 9–1.30 💶 Inexpensive

What to See in Northern Central Italy

ANCONA

The capital of the province of Le Marche (The Marches) was
founded on the Adriatic coast in the 4th or 5th century BC.
Survivors from its early history include a fine collection of Hellenic,
Etruscan and Roman art and artefacts in the **Museo Archeologico
Nazionale delle Marche** and the well-preserved Arco di Traiano
(Trajan's Arch, AD115) overlooking the port. Several later historic
monuments survived heavy World War II bombing; among these
are the 15th-century Loggia dei Mercanti, with a Gothic façade,
and 10th-century Santa Maria della Piazza, with floor mosaics from
an earlier church on the same site.

✚ 135 A5
Museo Archeologico Nazionale delle Marche
✉ Palazzo Ferretti, Via Ferretti 6 ☎ 071 202 602 🕐 Tue–Sun 8.30–7.30.
Closed 1 Jan, 1 May, 25 Dec ✋ Moderate

AREZZO

Originally a major Etruscan and Roman centre, Arezzo preserves
remains from its ancient past in the **Museo Archeologico**
overlooking a 1st-century Roman amphitheatre. Over the years,
the city's many illustrious sons have included the poet Petrarch
(1304–74), and the artist Giorgio Vasari (1511–74), who built,
decorated and lived in **Casa di Vasari.** He also contributed to work
on the **Pieve (parish church) di Santa Maria.** Arezzo's main
crowd-puller is the church of **San Francesco,** with Piero della
Francesca's magnificent frescoes (1452–66). These illustrate the
life story of Christ's cross from its origins in the Garden of Eden
to its final rediscovery and rescue by St Helena, mother of the
emperor Constantine. The **Museo d'Arte Medievale e Moderna**
has a good collection of 14th- to 19th-century Tuscan art.
✚ 134 A3
Museo Archeologico
✉ Via Margaritone 10 ☎ 0575 20 882 🕐 Daily 8.30–7.30 ✋ Moderate
Casa di Vasari
✉ Via XX Settembre 55 ☎ 0575 409 040 🕐 Mon, Wed–Sat 9–7, Sun 9–1
✋ Inexpensive
Pieve di Santa Maria
✉ Corso Italia 🕐 Daily 8–1, 3–6.30
San Francesco
www.pierodellafrancesca.it
✉ Piazza San Francesco ☎ 0575 900 404 🕐 Mon–Sat 9–6, Sun 1–5.30
(later in summer). Reservations essential (☎ 0575 352 727) ✋ Moderate
Museo d'Arte Medievale e Moderna
✉ Via di San Lorentino 8 ☎ 0575 409 050 🕐 Tue–Sun 9–7. Closed public
hols ✋ Inexpensive

ASCOLI PICENO

The medieval historic centre of this walled town more or less follows the grid street plan of the old Roman Asculum Picenum. At its heart lies Piazza del Popolo, whose highlights are the 13th-century Palazzo dei Capitani del Popolo, the church of San Francesco (1258–1549), and the adjoining Loggia dei Mercanti (1513) where merchants carried out their business. On stately old Piazza dell'Arringo there is a 12th-century Duomo, with another Amatrice façade, a Carlo Crivelli polyptych (1473) inside and a splendid 12th-century baptistery.

✚ 135 B5

ASSISI

Assisi was at the heart of a series of earthquakes that shook central Italy in the autumn of 1997. Some important historic buildings were damaged, including the **Basilica di San Francesco,** St Francis's burial place and Assisi's most important monument. Started in 1228, this magnificent church contained matchless frescoes by Giotto, Cimabue, Lorenzetti and others. A few of

these were virtually destroyed, but have since been magnificently restored. Other monuments include the 12th- and 13th-century Romanesque **Duomo** huddled next to its hefty campanile; the impressively positioned 14th-century castle, the **Rocca Maggiore;** many small churches and the church of **Santa Chiara,** with Giotto-influenced interior frescoes. Assisi's oldest monument, the 1st-century BC Tempio di Minerva (converted into a church), on the attractive Piazza del Comune, escaped the earthquake unscathed.

www.comune.assisi.pg.it; www.assisionline.com

✚ 134 A4

Basilica di San Francesco

✉ Piazza San Francesco ☎ 075 819 001 ⏰ Apr–Sep daily 7–7; Oct–Mar daily 7–5. Closed public hols 👊 Inexpensive

Duomo

✉ Piazza San Ruffino

Rocca Maggiore

✉ Via Maria delle Rose

⏰ Daily 9 to sunset

Santa Chiara

✉ Piazza Santa Chiara

CORTONA

This perfect example of a Tuscan hilltown was founded by the Etruscans, whose artefacts, along with other ancient remains, can be seen in the **Museo dell'Accademia Etrusca** in the Palazzo Pretorio, one of the late medieval civic buildings on Piazza della Repubblica. The Museo Diocesano, housed in a deconsecrated church, has works by Fra Angelico, Signorelli (who was born in Cortona) and others.

www.cortonaweb.com

✚ 134 A3

Museo dell'Accademia Etrusca

✉ Piazza Signorelli 19 ☎ 0575 630 415 ⏰ Apr–Sep Tue–Sun, 10–7; Oct–Mar Tue–Sun 10–5 👊 Moderate

ELBA

Napoleon was exiled on this lush little island after his 1814 abdication. He led a simple life from his country **Villa San Martino,** but an escape attempt led to exile for real on bleak St Helena in the Atlantic Ocean. Apart from enjoying the beautiful bays, cliffs, fishing villages and inland scenery, visitors today can admire the view from 1,000m (3,280ft) Monte Capanne and explore the museums in Portoferraio and Marciano.

✚ 134 B1 ⛴ from Piombino

Villa San Martino

✉ San Martino ☎ 0565 914 688 🕙 Mon, Wed–Sat 9–7, Sun 9–1. Closed 1 Jan, 25 Dec 👤 Inexpensive

GUBBIO

Clinging to the lower slopes of Monte Ingino, this enchanting Umbrian town has remained essentially unchanged since the Middle Ages. Along its winding streets of heavy, full-bodied houses are mysterious narrow doorways, evocatively called *porte della morte* (doors of death). The main monuments include the hefty Palazzo dei Consoli (1332), whose Museo Civico has 3rd-century BC Etruscan-inscribed tablets; the Palazzo Ducale (1470), with its fine Renaissance courtyard; the Gothic **Duomo;** and the 13th-century church of **San Francesco,** with frescoes (1404–13) by Ottaviano Nelli. The stage-like, elevated Piazza della Signoria (or Piazza Grande) is on a man-made platform. Every year on 15 May, three vast, wooden 'ceri' (candles), each 4m (13ft) long, are raced by competing teams through Gubbio and up to the church of Sant'Ubaldo on top of 820m (2,690ft) Monte Ingino.

You can see them in the church by climbing the mountain or taking the cable-car from Porta Romana.

www.gubbioweb.it

✚ 134 A4

Duomo

✉ Via Ducale

San Francesco

✉ Piazza 40 Martiri

MAREMMA

Italy's answer to the Wild West, where *butteri* (cowboys) herd docile horned cattle and stage rodeo shows, lies along the coast of southern Tuscany. The rest of this area of mainland low hills falls within the **Parco Regionale dell'Uccellina,** with marked footpaths and picnic areas. The evocative ruins of defence towers, built by the Medici in the 16th century, overlook the Maremma's wide, undeveloped beaches. To its north lie salt marshes.

✚ 134 B2 🚆 and 🚌 To Grosseto

Parco Regionale dell'Uccellina

✉ Centro Visite di Alberese

☎ 0564 407 098 🕐 Daily 8.30–sunset

ORVIETO

Orvieto sits on top of a volcanic outcrop and is famous for its wine. The Duomo (13th–16th centuries) is one of the finest in Italy, its dazzling façade a mass of mosaics, sculpture and bas-reliefs with modern bronze doors by Emilio Greco (1969). The highlights of the interior are the Cappella Nuova frescoes by Signorelli (1499). Other unmissables in Orvieto include the nearby **Museo Claudio Faina;** the Pozzo di San Patrizio, a 62m-deep (203ft) well (1527) with two staircases spiralling around its side; and the 13th-century Palazzo del Popolo.
www.orvietoturismo.it

✚ 134 B3

Museo Claudio Faina

✉ Piazza del Duomo 29 ☎ 0763 341 511 🕐 Apr–Sep daily, 9.30–6;
Oct–Mar Tue–Sun 10–5. Closed 1 Jan, 25–26 Dec 👆 Moderate

PERUGIA

The outskirts of Perugia are a modern, urban sprawl, but the city centre is pure Medieval and Renaissance, focused on the dramatic Piazza IV Novembre and its 13th-century Fontana Maggiore. Also on the piazza are the Palazzo dei Priori (13th century), its inner walls frescoed by Cavallini (1273–1308), Perugino (1445–1523) and others, and the Gothic Cathedral with a baroque doorway. The **Galleria Nazionale d'Umbria** has the region's best collection of 13th- to 18th-century art. Elsewhere in the city, important

monuments include the Museo Archeologico Nazionale dell'Umbria; and the serene Oratorio di San Bernardino (1457–61), with bas-reliefs by Agostino di Duccio.

✚ 134 A4

Galleria Nazionale d'Umbria

www.gallerianazionaledellumbria.it

✉ Corso Vannucci ☎ 075 572 1009, 199 101 330 ◷ Daily 8.30–7. Closed 1st Mon of month, public hols ✋ Expensive

PISA

Pisa's most famous landmark, the 54m (177ft) **Leaning Tower (Torre Pendente),** was leaning so much (about 5.5m/18ft) that it was closed to the public from 1990 until 2001 for major restoration. Built between 1173 and 1350 as the Duomo's campanile, it started to lean in 1274. It is one of four dreamlike monuments on the surreally perfect Campo dei Miracoli (Piazza del Duomo). Buscheto started the Duomo in 1064. Inside are a pulpit (1302–11) carved by Pisano and mosaics (1302) by Cimabue. There is another carved pulpit in the Battistero (12th–13th centuries) with Gothic decoration by Pisano. Although the Camposanto cemetery was badly bombed in World War II, traces of its 14th-century frescoes have survived. The Museo Nazionale di San Matteo houses 13th- to 17th-century Tuscan art, notably works by Andrea Pisano; Piazza dei Cavalieri has many Renaissance buildings by Vasari; and Santa Maria della Spina (1230–1323) is a sugary Gothic creation rebuilt on its present site in 1871 to avoid flooding.

www.pisaturismo.it

✚ 133 F5

Torre Pendente

✉ Campo dei Miracoli ☎ 050 560 547 ◷ Apr–Sep daily 8–8; Mar, Oct daily 9–8; Nov–Feb daily 9–5 ✋ Expensive ❓ Buy tickets online or in advance from the ticket office at the tower

PISTOIA

The heart of Pistoia's walled historic centre is Piazza del Duomo, with the 14th-century Gothic Battistero and the 12th- to 13th-century Duomo, both in striped dark and light marble. Inside the Duomo is the silver altar of St James (1287–1456). Further afield lie the churches of Sant'Andrea (12th century), with pulpit and crucifix (1298–1308) by Giovanni Pisano, and San Giovanni Fuorcivitas (12th–14th centuries), on Via Cavour, with a Taddeo Gaddi polyptych and a Luca della Robbia terracotta. The Ospedale del Ceppo, on Piazza Giovanni XXII, has a unique terracotta frieze by Luca's great-nephew, Giovanni della Robbia.

✚ 133 E5

SAN GALGANO

The romantic skeleton of a 13th-century abbey, dissolved in the 17th century, lies surrounded by lush trees and fields between Siena and Massa Marittima. It was built by Cistercian monks in French Gothic style, and its soothing, grassy remains give an insight into how such buildings were constructed. Overlooking the abbey is the circular Cappella di Montesiepi, containing a sword miraculously thrust into rock by St Galgano and frescoes of scenes from the saint's life (1344) by Ambrogio Lorenzetti.

✚ 134 A2 🚌 Bus from Siena

SAN GIMIGNANO

The skyline of San Gimignano, one of the prettiest and most visited medieval hilltowns in Tuscany, is dominated by 13 towers erected in the 12th and 13th centuries. At its heart lie Piazza della Cisterna, with a lovely medieval well, and Piazza del Duomo, where the 12th- to 13th-century **Collegiata** contains magnificent art by Ghirlandaio (1448–94) and others. There is more exceptional early Renaissance art in the Museo Civico, housed in the 13th-century Palazzo del Popolo, whose 54m-high (177ft) tower is the

town's tallest. The 13th-century church of Sant'Agostino has frescoes by Benozzo Gozzoli among its impressive artworks.
www.sangimignano.com

🕂 134 A2 🛈 Piazza Duomo 1 ☎ 0577 940 008

Collegiata

✉ Piazza del Duomo ☎ 0577 942 226 🕐 Mar–Oct Mon–Fri 9.30–7.30, Sat 9.30–5, Sun 1–5; Nov–Feb Mon–Sat 9.30–5, Sun 1–5 ✋ Moderate

SAN MARINO

The capital of this independent little republic, which issues its own coins and postage stamps and has its own splendidly uniformed army and police force, is perched on a precipitous cliff, with vertiginous views from the footpath that links its three picture-book **Rocche** (castles); one of them contains a museum of arms.

🕂 133 E7 🚌 Access by bus

Rocche

🕐 Jun–Sep daily 8–8; Oct–May daily 9–5 ✋ Inexpensive

SIENA

Winding streets of dignified medieval and Renaissance
buildings open out on to the main Piazza del Campo, a
dramatic, sloping, shell-shaped piazza with the 13th- to
14th-century Palazzo Pubblico at its foot. Inside the
palazzo is the **Museo Civico,** whose frescoes of *Good
and Bad Government* (Lorenzetti, 1338–40) symbolize the
philosophy of this civilized city. Towering over the *palazzo*
is the 102m (334ft) Torre del Mangia (1138), with
excellent views at the top of its 505 stairs. Every
summer competing local teams, each wearing different
colours, race horses round the *campo* in the *Palio* (➤ 11).
Behind the opulent façade of the Duomo (1136–1382)
lies a wealth of art treasures, including Pinturicchio
frescoes (1509) in the Piccolomini Library, a font by della
Quercia and Donatello, and a magnificent marble inlaid

floor. The Museo dell'Opera del Duomo, the Ospedale di Santa Maria della Scala and the Pinacoteca Nazionale contain other important artworks. Civic relics from Siena's past are on display in the Palazzo Piccolomini (1460s). Siena's (and one of Italy's) patron saints, St Catherine of Siena (1347–80), dedicated herself to God at the age of eight and became a holy mystic. Her house (Via Camporeggio 37) is full of illustrations of her life while her preserved head is in the church of San Domenico (1226 onwards), along with various frescoes.

www.terresiena.it

➕ 134 A2

Museo Civico

☎ 0577 292 232 ⏱ Daily 10–7 ✋ Expensive

SPOLETO

This breathtaking Umbrian town contains relics from a history that dates back to pre-

Roman times. These include the 1st-century BC Arco di Druso (Arch of Drusus), in Piazza del Mercato, and the monumental Ponte delle Torri (Bridge of Towers), built in the 12th century over the remains of a Roman aqueduct. The graceful façade of the 12th-century **Duomo** has no fewer than eight rose windows; the restored, largely 17th-century interior includes works by Bernini, Pinturicchio and Carracci.

➕ 134 B4

Duomo

✉ Piazza del Duomo

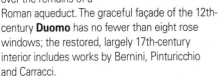

TODI

Spilling over the edge of its hilltop location, this pretty town is notable for its medieval architecture. Piazza del Popolo, at its heart, is the setting for the 13th-century Palazzo del Capitano, Palazzo del Priori and Palazzo del Popolo, housing the restored **Museo Etrusco-Romano and Pinacoteca** (picture gallery). The regal Romanesque-Gothic Duomo contains fine Renaissance stalls, while the church of San Fortunato is a pleasing mix of Gothic and Renaissance, with frescoes (1432) by Masolino. One of the best gems of the Italian Renaissance, the church of Santa Maria della Consolazione (probably planned by Bramante), lies on the Orvieto road, on the outskirts of Todi.

✚ 134 B4

Museo Etrusco-Romano and Pinacoteca

✉ Piazza del Popolo ☎ 075 895 6216 🕐 Apr–Aug Tue–Sun 10.30–1, 2.30–6; Oct–Feb Tue–Sun 10.30–1, 2–4.30; Mar, Sep Tue–Sun 10.30–1, 2–5. Closed Mon except Apr ✋ Moderate

URBINO

The Renaissance genius Raphael (1483–1520) was born here. One of the few works he left to his home town is in the **Galleria Nazionale delle Marche,** housed in the Renaissance Palazzo Ducale (1444–82), alongside other masterpieces by the likes of Lucca della Robbia, Uccello and Piero della Francesca; the Casa di Raffaello

contains only copies of Raphael's paintings. The Duomo was rebuilt by Valadier after an earthquake in 1789. The oratories of San Giuseppe (16th century) and San Giovanni Battista (late 14th century) are also worth visiting; the first for its fine crib and the second for frescoes (1416) by brothers Giacomo and Lorenzo Salimbeni.

➕ 133 F7

Galleria Nazionale delle Marche

✉ Piazza Duca Federico ☎ 0722 329 057 🕐 Mon 8.30–2, Tue–Sun 8.30–7:15. Closed 1 Jan, 1 May, 25 Dec 💷 Moderate

VOLTERRA

This is one of the best places to see Etruscan remains. These include parts of the Arco Etrusco (the rest is Roman) and the unrivalled **Museo Etrusco Guarnacci**'s collection. There is also a fine 1st-century BC Roman theatre. Other sights include excellent 14th- to 17th-century Tuscan art in the Pinacoteca and Museo Civico; austere 13th-century *palazzi* on Piazza dei Priori; and a Romanesque Duomo, with 13th-century sculpture and baptistery and 12th-century bas-reliefs on the 17th-century pulpit.

www.volterratour.it

➕ 134 A2

Museo Etrusco Guarnacci

✉ Via Don Minzoni 15 ☎ 0588 86 347 🕐 Mid-Mar to Oct 9–6.45; Nov to mid-Mar 9–1. Closed 1 Jan, 25 Dec 💷 Expensive (includes entrance to Pinacoteca)

Southern Central Italy

This is the area in which the rich, cosmopolitan north meets the more traditional, mellow *mezzogiorno* (south) – not just geographically but culturally and gastronomically as well.

The best place to see the resulting blend of cut-and-thrust northern Europe with the slower paced Mediterranean way of life is Rome, where politicians and business people rush through sun-soaked piazzas and strolling crowds.

Apart from Rome and its immediate vicinity, south central Italy is slightly off the tourist track and even the beaches, while just as well developed as those elsewhere in Italy, don't attract the same international crowd, catering instead to hordes of weekenders from nearby towns and cities.

To the east of Rome lie the rugged mountains of Abruzzo and Molise. Here, age-old isolated communities serve as centres for hillwalking in summer and skiing in winter.

Roma (Rome)

Italy's capital has almost 3,000 years of history packed into the narrow, winding streets and majestic *piazzas* of its historic centre. Its greatest monuments include the civic and religious head-quarters of an ancient empire, churches founded during the earliest days of Christianity, and pompous baroque palaces built for the powerful noble families who amassed vast collections of works by the great artists they patronized.

✚ 134 C4

ℹ Via Parigi 5 ☎ 06 4889 9253; www.romaturismo.it

BASILICA DI SAN PIETRO AND IL VATICANO
See pages 22–23.

BOCCA DELLA VERITÀ
In the portico of the 12th-century church of Santa Maria in Cosmedin (note the fine inlaid Cosmati marble pavement inside) is a strange, ancient marble face (originally a drain cover) with an open mouth. Legend has it that the mouth of truth will clamp shut on the hand of anybody who lies – during the Middle Ages it was a common test of wives' marital fidelity. Across the road are the rectangular temple of Portunus from the 2nd century BC and the round temple of Hercules from the 1st century BC.

✚ 139 E5 ✉ Santa Maria in Cosmedin, Via Teatro di Marcello 🚌 81, 160, 715

CAMPIDOGLIO

Michelangelo designed Rome's magnificent civic centre, which today houses the mayor's office in the Palazzo Senatorio and the **Musei Capitolini** in the flanking *palazzi* Nuovo and dei Conservatori. The central *piazza* contains a copy of the 2nd-century AD statue of Marcus Aurelius. Highlights of the main museum include the sensual *Dying Gaul*, the delightful 1st-century BC *Spinario* (a bronze of a boy extracting a thorn from his foot) and the *She-Wolf Suckling Romulus and Remus* (symbol of Rome). The picture gallery has works by Caravaggio, Guercino, Pietro da Cortona, Guido Reni, Tintoretto and others. In the late 1990s the museums underwent a major renovation and some of the priceless ancient statues were transferred to the incongruous yet atmospheric surroundings of a former electricity power plant near Ostiense station, the Central Montemartini, where Roman heads, creamy Venuses and other works are exhibited next to obsolete industrial machinery.

✚ 139 E5

Musei Capitolini

✉ Piazza del Campidoglio ☎ 06 3996 7800; www.museicapitolini.org 🕐 Tue–Sun 9–8 💰 Expensive 🚌 40, 60, 86, 88, 590, 715

CASTEL SANT'ANGELO

Built by Emperor Hadrian (AD117–138) as a mausoleum for himself, the *castel* was used as a defensive stronghold by generations of popes from the Middle Ages until the unification of Italy. Since 1886 it has been open to the public, who enter via the original ramp used by Hadrian's funeral procession. Other highlights include a courtyard with Montelupo's statue of an angel (1544) sheathing a sword, and a Michelangelo gateway (1514). Off the courtyard are the delicately frescoed, 16th-century state rooms including the Sala di Apollo, where holes in the floor lead to notorious prisons, and the magnificent Sala Paolina, with a delightfully enigmatic *trompe l'oeil* door. There are good views over Rome from the ramparts.

🚩 138 C3 ✉ Lungotevere Castello 50 ☎ 06 681 9111
🕐 Tue–Sun 9–7 👊 Moderate 🚌 23, 40, 64

FORO ROMANO, PALATINO AND COLOSSEO
See pages 30–31.

GALLERIA BORGHESE

The sculpture, on the ground floor, includes important classical works (*Sleeping Hermaphrodite, Dancing Faun*) and Canova's famous sculpture of Napoleon's sister, Pauline Bonaparte Borghese, as a seductive Venus. The highlights, however, are the spectacular early sculptures by Bernini, showing his precocious talent in works such as *The Rape of Proserpine*. Among the celebrated paintings on the ground-floor walls and upstairs are a *Deposition* by Raphael; Titian's early masterpiece, *Sacred and Profane Love*; a rich, vibrant *Last Supper* by Jacopo Bassano; and Correggio's erotic *Danaë*. The six Caravaggio paintings include his important early work, the luscious *Boy with a Fruit Basket*.

✚ 139 A7 ✉ Piazzale Scipione Borghese 5, Villa Borghese ☎ 06 854 8577 ◑ Tue–Sat 9–7; reservations compulsory ✋ Expensive ▣ 52, 53, 910

PALAZZO ALTEMPS

This lovingly restored baroque *palazzo* is the perfect setting for the vast ancient sculpture collection amassed in the 16th century by Prince Ludovisi. The prince hired some of the best sculptors of his own time (including Bernini and Algardi) to patch up damaged specimens among his newly acquired Greek and Roman masterpieces. Some of the results are ridiculous, with spare heads and limbs spliced on to unmatching torsos. However, even the most demanding ancient-art purists will delight in the Aldovisi Throne, a serene 5th-century BC portrayal of the goddess Aphrodite.

✚ 138 C4 ✉ Piazza Sant'Apollinare 44 ☎ 06 683 3759 ◑ Tue–Sun 9–7.45 ✋ Moderate ▣ 70, 81, 87, 115, 116, 186, 492, 628

PALAZZO BARBERINI

A national art gallery since 1949, this is one of Rome's grandest baroque palaces – Carlo Maderno, Bernini and Borromini all worked on its exterior, while its sumptuous interior includes an elaborate ceiling fresco by Pietro da Cortona in the *Gran Salone*. The collection gives a good overview of (principally Italian) 13th- to 17th-century painting but excels in its 16th- and 17th-century paintings by the likes of Andrea del Sarto, Raphael, Bernini, El Greco, Bronzino, Guido Reni, Guercino and Caravaggio.

➕ 139 C6 ✉ Via Quattro Fontane 13 ☎ 06 32810 🕘 Tue–Sun 9–7
✋ Moderate 🚌 60, 61, 62, 175, 492, 590

PALAZZO DORIA PAMPHILJ

This has been the seat of the noble Roman family of Doria Pamphilj since the late Renaissance. In the grand reception rooms and picture galleries, with their elaborate frescoed ceilings, the paintings are hung exactly as they were in the 18th century, cluttered side by side from floor to ceiling. They include works by Memling, Raphael, Titian, Tintoretto and Caravaggio. The star of the collection is Velásquez's portrait of Pope Innocent X, resplendent in vermilion robes.

www.doriapamphilj.it

➕ 139 D5 ✉ Piazza del Collegio Romano 2 ☎ 06 679 7323 🕘 Daily 10–5

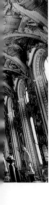

PANTHEON

Erected by Marcus Agrippa (1st century AD), this awe-inspiring temple to all the gods became a Christian church in 609 and contains the tombs of Raphael and Vittorio Emanuele II, the first king of united Italy. It is a miracle of ancient engineering: the massive semicircular dome, 43.3m (142ft) in diameter, was constructed by pouring concrete over a wooden framework. The huge bronze doors are ancient Roman, the ornate marble floor is a 19th-century reconstruction of the original, and the subtly vibrant colours of its interior have been restored.

✚ 139 D5 ✉ Piazza della Rotonda ☎ 06 6830 0230 ⏱ Mon–Sat 8.30–6 (7.30 in summer), Sun 9–5.30 🚌 116 to Via della Palombella

PIAZZA NAVONA

One of the world's most beautiful squares owes its elongated shape to the 1st-century AD stadium over which it was built (remains lie to its north). The piazza's centrepiece is Bernini's spectacular *Fontana dei Fiumi* (1651), featuring symbolic representations of the rivers Ganges, Danube, Plate and Nile clinging to a massive artificial cliff-face, in front of the church of Sant'Agnese in Agone (the work of, among others, Bernini's great rival Borromini). The figure at the centre of the fountain to the southeast is also by Bernini.

✚ 138 D4 🚌 70, 81, 87, 115, 116, 186, 492, 628

a walk in Rome's historic centre

Combine this walk with visits to the Forum (► 30) and St Peter's and the Vatican (► 22–23) and you can claim to have 'done' Rome.

From Largo Argentina follow the Corso Vittorio Emanuele II to Via Paradiso (left) and head into the pretty market place, Campo de' Fiori.

From here enter Piazza della Cancelleria, where Palazzo della Cancelleria (1485–1513) contains papal offices.

Turn right on Corso Vittorio Emanuele II; cross at the lights at the Museo Baracco (ancient sculpture). Continue down Via Cuccagna into Piazza Navona (► 103). Along the piazza, Corso Agone leads right to Palazzo Madama.

This 16th-century palace is now the seat of the Senate. Via Salvatore runs alongside it to San Luigi dei Francesi (left), containing Caravaggio paintings.

Continue straight to the Pantheon (► 103). Turn right opposite the Pantheon into Vicolo della Maddalena, right down Via del Vicario into Piazza del Montecitorio (Parliament House). Follow Via di Guglia, in front of the palazzo, turning left at Via dei Pastini onto Piazza di Pietra (columns of a 2nd-century AD temple of

Hadrian). Follow Via di Pietra, cross Via del Corso and continue up Via di Muratte.

You come to the famous Trevi fountain (1762 by Nicola Salvi); throw in a coin if you want to return to Rome.

Follow Via della Stamperia, turn right up Via del Tritone, cross and turn left on Via Due Macelli to Piazza di Spagna.

Pause on the Spanish Steps before climbing them and turning left, past the 16th-century Villa Medici.

Take the path on the right to the Pincio. Continue down into Piazza del Popolo.

Santa Maria del Popolo church contains Caravaggio works.

Distance 4.5km (3 miles)
Time 1.5 hours without stops, 3–4 hours with stops
Start point Largo Argentina
✚ 139 D5
End point Piazza del Popolo
✚ 139 A5
🚇 Flaminio
Lunch Hostaria Romanesca (€)
✉ Campo de'Fiori 40

PIAZZA VENEZIA

Central Rome's hub is dominated by the white marble monument to Vittorio Emanuele II. To its left is the **Palazzo Venezia,** now a museum of applied arts. To its right are the remains of the 2nd-century AD Mercati Traianei (Trajan's Markets), behind Trajan's column and the Imperial Forums. They were built when the Forum could no longer handle the business of running Rome.

✚ 139 D5

Palazzo Venezia

✉ Via del Plebiscito 118 ☎ 06 6999 4319 ⏰ Tue–Sun 8.30–7 🖐 Moderate 🚌 44, 46, 84, 715, 810

SAN CLEMENTE

A tour of this three-layered building starts with a 12th-century church containing a contemporary apse mosaic, a 6th-century choir stall and Masolini frescoes of St Catherine of Alexandria. Beneath this is a 4th-century church containing 11th-century frescoes of St Clement and a large circular well, probably a font.

Below this are ancient Roman remains, including a cramped Mithraeum (temple of Mithras) with a small altar with a relief of Mithras slaying a bull. The route back up passes through the walls of ancient Roman apartment blocks.

🕂 139 E8 ✉ Via San Giovanni in Laterano ☎ 06 7045 1018 🕓 Mon–Sat 9–12.30, 3–6, Sun 10–12.30, 3–6 ✋ Inexpensive; upper church free 🚌 85, 167, 850

SAN GIOVANNI IN LATERANO

This was the home of the papacy from the 4th to the 14th centuries, and is now the Cathedral of Rome (the pope doubles up as Bishop of Rome). The building is 16th century with a portico (1585) by Fontana, façade by Galilei and nave (1650) by Borromini. Inside are remnants of earlier buildings, and 5th-century mosaics in the baptistery.

🕂 139 F8 (off map) ✉ Piazza San Giovanni in Laterano ☎ 06 7720 7991 🕓 Basilica: 7–7 (6 in winter); Baptistery: daily 7–12.30, 4–7.30; Cloisters: 9–6 (5 in winter) 🚌 30b, 81, 85, 87, 186, 590, 850

SANTA MARIA MAGGIORE

This hefty edifice has a ceiling clad in some of the first gold to be brought back from the New World. The Cappelle Sistina (1585) and Paolina (1611) contain important artworks, but the basilica's main glory lies in its mosaics. In the nave is a 5th-century narrative of the Old Testament and, in the apse, an impressive *Glorification of Mary* (1295). The site of the church is said to have been decided by the Virgin sending an unseasonal fall of snow to this spot, an event still commemorated every August.

🕂 139 D8 ✉ Piazza di Santa Maria Maggiore ☎ 06 483 195 🕓 Summer 7–7; winter 9–5 🚌 16, 70, 71, 75, 204, 590

What to See in Southern Central Italy

CASTELLI ROMANI

The small medieval towns on the slopes of the Alban Hills are close enough to Rome to be reachable for lunch – or even dinner if you have a car and want to enjoy the lights of the city from afar. The white wines they produce are often served as *vino della casa* in Rome's restaurants and *trattorie*. Frascati, the nearest of the Castelli, is dominated by the **Villa Aldobrandini** (1598–1603), while Rocca di Papa is the highest (680m/2,230ft) and has fine medieval buildings; the main piazza of Ariccia is adorned by Bernini, and Albano Laziale has Etruscan and Roman ruins. The pope's summer residence is at **Castel Gandolfo.**

✚ 134 C4 (Frascati and Castel Gandolfo)

Villa Aldobrandini

✉ Piazzale Marconi, Frascati ☎ 06 942 0331 🕓 Mon–Fri 9–1, 3–6 (5 in winter)

Castel Gandolfo

✉ Piazza Plebiscito

ETRURIA

The region of Lazio settled by the Etruscans includes Tarquinia, 2km (1.2 miles) southeast of which are magnificent painted tombs in the Necropoli di Monterozzi. Tarquinia also has a well-stocked **Museo Nazionale.** Another major Etruscan centre is Cerveteri, where one of the highlights of the Necropoli di Banditaccia (2km/1.2 miles north) is the Tomb of the Reliefs, showing scenes from everyday Etruscan life. Vulci, Norchia and Tuscania also have Etruscan remains.

www.tarquinia.net

✚ 134 C3 (Tarquinia and Cerveteri)

Museo Nazionale di Tarquinia

✉ Piazza Cavour ☎ 0766 856 036 🕓 Tue–Sun 9–7. Closed public hols

✋ Expensive (includes visit to necropolis)

L'AQUILA

Gran Sasso (2,914m/9,557ft), the highest of the Apennines, towers above the capital of Abruzzo and can best be seen from the majestic 16th-century Castello, which now houses the **Museo Nazionale d'Abruzzo** with its fine collection of art from ancient to modern times. The symbolic Fontana delle 99 Cannelle (Fountain of the 99 Spouts, 1272, but much restored since) has a spout for each of the communities involved in the city's founding in 1240.

Other prime monuments are the churches of Santa Maria di Collemaggio (started in 1287), with its pink and white geometric façade (14th century), and San Bernardino (1454–72), whose 17th-century restoration includes a baroque ceiling.

www.regione.abruzzo.it;
www.parks.it

✚ 135 C5

Museo Nazionale d'Abruzzo

✉ Castello Cinquecentesco
☎ 0862 6331 ◷ Tue–Sun 9–8.
Closed public hols 💷 Moderate

OSTIA ANTICA

Although nothing like as complete as Pompei (► 36–37), this ancient Roman port (now a long way from the sea) has some fine remains dating from the 1st century BC to the 4th century AD. These stand in a pretty area of encroaching vegetation that creates a park-like atmosphere. Highlights include the mosaics of the Piazzale delle Corporazioni, representing the trading interests of the corporations whose offices stood here; the thermopolium, where hot food and drinks were served (note the illustrated, frescoed menu); the nearby Casa di Diana apartment block; the Terme di Nettuno baths; and a theatre.

www.ostiaantica.net

✚ 134 C3 ✉ Via Romagnoli 717, Ostia Antica ☎ 06 5635 8099 🕓 Apr–Sep Tue–Sun 8.30–7.30; Oct–Mar Tue–Sun 8.30–4 ✋ Moderate 🚇 Metro from Rome

PARCO NAZIONALE D'ABRUZZO

These 40,000ha (98,840 acres) of mountain wilderness are covered with dense beech and maple forests and shelter many wild animals, including about 100 Marsican brown bears,

Apennine wolves, golden eagles, Abruzzo chamois and wild cats. (If you don't spot these in the wild, you can go to the zoo near the park's headquarters to see convalescing injured animals.) The park is well laid out with marked trails, picnic areas and campsites.
www.parcoabruzzo.it; www.parks.it

✚ 135 C5 ✉ Headquarters: Via Consultore 1, Pescasseroli ☎ 0863 91 955
🚌 Bus from Avezzano or Alfedena

TIVOLI

Most people come to this hillside town to see the spectacular terraced gardens of the **Villa d'Este** (1550), where the statuary, including a row of grotesque heads spitting water, outdoes the plant life. Nearby are the stately remains of the Villa Adriana. Built for Emperor Hadrian between AD118 and 134, this is a vast area of ruined follies, including a massive fishpond, the circular Teatro Marittimo on an island in an artificial lake, and many nymphaeums. There are also temples, barracks and a museum.

✚ 134 C4 🚌 Bus from Rome

Villa d'Este

✉ Piazza Trento, Tivoli ☎ 0774 333 404 🕐 Tue–Sun 8.30 to one hour before sunset 🎫 Expensive

Southern Italy, Sardinia and Sicily

The summer sun rules supreme in the _mezzogiorno_ (the south), giving everything an added intensity: colours are brighter, sounds are louder, and flavours richer and more pungent. With the exception of Naples, the Costiera Amalfitana and parts of Sardinia and Sicily, this region is off the international tourist track, so there is plenty to discover.

The landscape varies from hostile mountains in Basilicata to flat, fertile plains in Puglia and dramatic photogenic coasts in Campania and Calabria. In addition, both the mainland and the islands of Sardinia and Sicily are full of reminders of a long history and centuries of foreign occupation from all corners of Europe and the Mediterranean.

South Italy is dotted with prehistoric, Greek and Roman ruins, Norman, Byzantine and Romanesque cathedrals, and effervescent baroque _palazzi_ of a lighter, less pompous style than that of their contemporaries to the north.

Napoli (Naples)

You either love Naples or hate it; no visitor remains indifferent. This chaotic city, and its exuberant inhabitants, living on the coast beneath Vesuvius, have a character all of their own. In the 18th and 19th centuries, Naples was one of the main stops on the Grand Tour, but during the 20th century crumbling architecture and a soaring crime rate sent the city into decline. A major clean-up programme has greatly improved the situation, but it's still worth taking particular care of your valuables here.

✚ 136 B2

ℹ️ Piazza dei Martiri 58 ☎ 081 405 311; www.inaples.it

CASTEL NUOVO AND PALAZZO REALE

This pleasing caricature of a castle, with crenellations and stolid chess-piece towers, was rebuilt in the 15th century over a 12th-century original. Its majestic entrance is based on ancient Roman triumphal arches. Inside is the 14th-century Cappella Palatina (from the previous building), the

Museo Civico and 14th- to 18th-century art. The nearby **Palazzo Reale** was the Bourbon royal residence from 1734 to 1860. It contains antique furniture, a library of historic manuscripts, and Neapolitan frescoes (17th–18th centuries).

Castel Nuovo

✉ Piazza Municipio ☎ 081 795 5877 🕐 Mon–Sat 9–7
💷 Moderate

Palazzo Reale

✉ Piazza Plebiscito ☎ 081 580 811 🕐 Thu–Tue 9–9.
Closed early Mar, public hols 💷 Moderate

CERTOSA DI SAN MARTINO AND CASTEL SANT'ELMO

On a hill with fine views over Naples' historic centre and the bay, this gem of Neapolitan baroque has aristocratic cloisters by Cosimo Fanzago, an opulent, marble-inlaid

church and a fascinating museum of traditional Christmas cribs, maps, art, and artefacts illustrating the history of Naples. Behind it stands the star-shaped Castel Sant'Elmo (14th century, rebuilt in the 16th), used as a prison in the 18th century and during the Risorgimento (19th century).

✉ Largo di San Martino 1 ☎ 081 578 1769 🕐 Tue–Sun
9–7.30 💷 Inexpensive

MUSEO ARCHEOLOGICO NAZIONALE

If nothing else brings you to Naples, come for this stupendous mass of ancient Greek and Roman artefacts, one of the best such collections in the world. Among treasures too numerous to list are the largest surviving ancient group sculpture (*Amphion and Zethus Tying Dirce to the Horns of the Bull*, 200BC, from the extensive Farnese collection); some of the most beautiful frescoes, mosaics and other artworks from Pompei (➤ 36–37) and Herculaneum (➤ 121); portrait busts of great Greeks and Romans; and rooms dedicated to erotic art.

✉ Piazza Museo Nazionale 19 ☎ 081 440 166 🕔 Wed–Mon 9–8
✋ Expensive

MUSEO DI CAPODIMONTE

Naples' most important art gallery is housed in an 18th-century royal hunting lodge. This is one of the best collections in Italy, with Renaissance and baroque masterpieces (by Masaccio, Bernini, Correggio, Titian, Pieter Brueghel and others), and an interesting section with 19th-century Neapolitan painting.

✉ Via di Miano 1, Parco di Capodimonte ☎ 081 749 9111 🕐 Thu–Tue 8.30–7.30 💷 Expensive

QUARTIERI SPAGNOLI

This grid of narrow streets below the Certosa di San Martino (► 115) was laid out by Spanish troops in the 17th century and is now a busy, inner-city residential area full of the sounds of people going about their day, and airing laundry – quintessential Naples, as seen in the movies.

✉ West of Via Toledo

SAN LORENZO MAGGIORE AND SAN GREGORIO ARMENO

Behind an 18th-century baroque façade lies the cool, simple Gothic interior of **San Lorenzo Maggiore** (14th century), whose tall, slender apse leads the eye automatically upwards. The Gothic mosaic-decorated tomb of Catherine of Austria (died 1323) is here. **San Gregorio Armeno,** around the corner, is a different story with its over-the-top baroque voluptuousness, which includes frescoes by Luca Giordano. The Benedictine convent attached to the church was a favourite among those daughters of the Neapolitan aristocracy who wished (or were forced) to take the veil.

San Lorenzo Maggiore
✉ Via Tribunali 316
San Gregorio Armeno
✉ Via San Gregorio Armeno 1

What to See in Southern Italy, Sardinia and Sicily

ALBEROBELLO

This beguiling little town makes the most of its role as the capital of *trulli* country. *Trulli* are the small white buildings with uncemented grey, conical stone roofs that have punctuated the landscape of central Puglia for centuries (although most of the ones you see today are at most 200 years old). As well as its streets of *trulli* homes (many of whose owners are only too happy to give you a guided tour), Alberobello boasts the *trullo* church of Sant'Antonio and the **Trullo Sovrano,** a museum devoted to the *trulli*.

✚ 137 B6

Trullo Sovrano

✉ Piazza Sacramento ☎ 080 432 6030 ◷ Apr–Oct daily 10–6 🎟 Inexpensive

BARI

The capital of Puglia has a labyrinthine historic centre in which the most impressive sights are the imposing **Castello** (1233), whose interesting interior contains casts of other Pugliese monuments, and the Basilica di San Nicola (1087), the first Norman church in the region and much copied elsewhere. The basilica's treasures include a fine 11th-century bishop's throne. One of the buildings based on San Nicola was Bari's

Romanesque cathedral (12th–13th centuries), whose interior remains essentially medieval behind a baroque façade.

➕ 137 A5

Castello

✉ Piazza Federico II di Svevia ☎ 080 528 6111 ⏰ Tue–Sun 8.30–7
👋 Inexpensive

BRINDISI

An important port since Roman times, this slightly drab city today swarms with backpackers and tourists on their way to the many Greece-bound ferries. The Roman column near the port marked the end of Via Appia, which has its beginning in Rome. Brindisi is not the most beautiful city in Italy, but its historic centre does have a certain run-down charm, and there are some good ancient vases in the **Museo Archeologico** opposite the Duomo.

➕ 137 B7

Museo Archeologico

✉ Piazza del Duomo 8 ☎ 0831 221 401 ⏰ Mon–Fri 9–1, 3–6, Sun 9–1
👋 Free

CAPRI

During the day, this beautiful island turns into an anthill of activity as daytrippers are shunted around in a continuous stream of minibuses taking in sights that include the sculpted Faraglioni rocks off the northeast coast, the soothing Certosa di San Giacomo (14th century) in Capri town, and the cable-car from Anacapri to the island's highest point. The highlight, however, is the famous **Grotta Azzurra** (Blue Grotto) where little boats, packed like sardine tins, whoosh through a low opening into the extraordinary sea-filled hollow in the cliff-face.

www.capri.net

✚ 136 B2 🚢 Ferry from Naples, boats from Sorrento and other towns on the Costiera Amalfitana (➤ 26–27)

Grotta Azzurra

🚢 Boat from Marina Grande in Capri harbour (not in rough weather)

💷 Expensive

CASTEL DEL MONTE

From the outside, this octagonal building with a tower on each of its corners resembles a massive sculpture. It was commissioned

by Emperor Frederick II in 1240 and is the most attractive and elaborate of the 200 fortresses he had built on his return from the Crusades. Inside, some of its plain, serene vaulted rooms are lined with marble, and there are wonderful views from the ramparts.

www.castellodelmonte.it (Italian only)

✚ 137 A5 ⊠ Località Andria, Bari
☎ 0883 569 997 🕐 Mar–Sep daily 10–7.30; Oct–Feb daily 9–6 👋 Inexpensive

COSTIERA AMALFITANA

See pages 26–27.

COSTIERA CALABRESE (CALABRIAN COAST)

The coast of Calabria has some of the cleanest water and most enticing beaches in Italy. Towns such as Scilla, Tropea, Maratea, Palmi and Pizzo are good centres from where to enjoy these, although a car is useful if you want to reach the quietest ones.

✚ 136 D4

ERCOLANO (HERCULANEUM)

The ancient city of Herculaneum (founded by the ancient Greeks) was buried by mud during the same eruption of Vesuvius that killed off Pompei (➤ 36–37). The excavations, while not as extensive as Pompei's, include some fine houses with mosaics, baths and a theatre.

✚ 136 B2 ⊠ Corso Ercolano, Ercolano ☎ 081 777 7008; www.pompeiisites.org 🕐 Daily 8.30am to one hour before sunset 👋 Expensive

GARGANO

To the northeast of Foggia is the beautiful Gargano promontory, 10,000ha (24,700 acres) of which is covered with the dense beech, pine and maple trees of the Foresta Umbra. White beaches and bays of turquoise water line its coast. The most scenic stretch of road is the one between Mattinata and the resort of Vieste, which has a 13th-century cathedral and from where boats leave to the equally undeveloped Isole Tremiti.

✚ 135 C8 🚌 Bus to Manfredonia, Vieste, Mattinata, Peschici and Rodi

LECCE

Founded by the Romans, and still retaining its 1st century amphitheatre, Lecce today is renowned as southern Italy's most perfect baroque city. Late Renaissance prosperity funded the building of churches and *palazzi*, constructed from the local sandstone. This was carved into elaborate decorative façades of intricate fruit, garlands and flowers, far lighter in design and spirit than northern baqoque. Santa Croce, the Duomo, the Rosario and the Palazzo del Governo are the finest examples.

✚ 137 B7

🛈 Corso Vitorrio Emanuele 24 ☎ 0832 24 80 92

MATERA

A handsome Puglian-Romanesque 13th-century **Duomo** stands at the top of this Basilicata city, but it is the strange lower town, the *sassi* district, that is most fascinating. This consists of buildings, including churches and a few *palazzi*, scooped out of the rock and closed off with normal façades. The cave-dwelling habit was probably started by 8th-century monks and continued well into the 20th century, although by then many *sassi* had become uninhabitable and their occupants were rehoused. Major restorations are under way to revive this eerie ghost town.

✚ 137 B5

Duomo

✉ Piazza del Duomo

PAESTUM

The 6th-century BC Greek city of Poseidonia was taken over by the Romans in 273BC and continued to be occupied until

malaria and the threat of Saracen attack led to its abandonment in the 9th century AD. Excavations, started in the 18th century, are among the most important in Italy. They include the temples of Neptune (5th century BC), Hera and Ceres (both 6th century BC), a stretch of city wall and a Roman forum. The museum has fine bas-reliefs among the other art and artefacts found on the site.

✚ 136 B3 ✉ Via Magna Grecia, Zona Archeologica, Paestum ☎ 0828 811 016 🕐 Daily 9 to one hour before sunset. Museum: 9–7. Closed 1st and 3rd Mon of month, public hols 💷 Moderate

POMPEI

See pages 36–37.

REGGIO DI CALABRIA

The main reason for venturing as far as this modern city in the toe of Italy (essentially rebuilt after an earthquake in 1908) is the **Museo Nazionale,** whose prime exhibits are two 5th-century BC Greek bronze statues of warriors, fished out of the sea in 1972. Highlights of the upstairs gallery include two 15th-century panel paintings by Antonello da Messina.

✚ 136 F4

Museo Nazionale

✉ Piazza de Nava 26 ☎ 0965 812 255 🕐 Daily 9–7.30. Closed 1st and 3rd Mon of month, public hols 👆 Moderate

SARDEGNA (SARDINIA)

Sardinia's Costa Smeralda (Emerald Coast) has some of the most fashionable beach resorts in Europe, but, if you avoid the glitzy jetset Porto Cervo, you don't have to be a millionaire to enjoy the limpid, turquoise waters that lap this fascinating island's shores. Among its many natural wonders are caves (especially the Grotta di Nettuno), the rugged islands of the Arcipelago della Maddalena, the barren, wild Monti del Gennargentu (rising to 1,800m/5,900ft), and the precipitous road between Arbatax and Dorgali.

Sardinia also has some of the oldest monuments in Europe: the unique *nuraghi* are conical buildings – of uncertain use – made out of blocks of stone and dating back as far as 1500BC. The best places to see *nuraghi* are Dorgali and Barumini. The island of Sant'Antioco has remains of the Phoenician and Roman settlement of Sulcis, and there are more Phoenician traces at Tharros. Remains from prehistoric and ancient Sardinia are in the

Museo Nazionale Archeologico in Cagliari, the enlarged island capital. The cathedral here has splendid 12th-century pulpits, carved by Guglielmo of Pisa with illustrations from the life of Christ. Sassari has the Museo Nazionale Sanna, another fine archaeological collection.

www.regione.sardegna.it

✚ 140 C3 (Cagliari) 🚢 Ferry from mainland to Cagliari, Olbia and Porto Torres ✈ Airports at Cagliari, Olbia and Alghero

Museo Nazionale Archeologico

✉ Cittadella dei Musei, Piazza Arsenale, Cagliari ☎ 070 684 000
🕐 Tue–Sun 9–8 ✋ Moderate

SICILIA (SICILY)

With a history during which Greek, Phoenician, Roman, Tunisian, Norman, French and Spanish occupations have all left their mark, Sicily has a culture and atmosphere that are subtly different from those of *il continente*, as mainland Italy is called here.

The vibrant city of **Palermo** is the capital. Its historic centre of crumbling baroque *palazzi* contains the Palazzo dei Normanni (Palace of the Normans) and the Cappella Palatina (Palatine Chapel), both with extraordinary Arab-Norman mosaics (12th century); the cathedral (12th to early 19th centuries); and the magnificent churches of La Martorana (Byzantine mosaics), San Giovanni degli Eremiti (Arab influenced) and San Cataldo (12th century). The Galleria Regionale della Sicilia has a major collection of Sicilian art, and the macabre Catacombe dei Cappuccini (Catacombs of the Capuchins) displays the clothed, mummified remains of 17th- to 19th-century Palermitani.

Near Palermo, the magnificently positioned Duomo at Monreale contains some of the most spectacular 12th- to 13th-century mosaics in existence. Segesta, to the west, has a splendid 5th-century BC temple and a 3rd-century BC theatre. East of Palermo, the pretty fishing village of Cefalù has a Norman

cathedral (1131–1240), with more mosaics, and southeast of here, in the middle of Sicily, is Piazza Armerina, where well-preserved mosaics in the Roman villa (3rd–4th century AD) include representations of scantily clad female athletes. **Siracusa** (Syracuse) has a spectacular archaeological area, spanning many centuries of the town's development, a medieval-baroque centre and the Museo Archeologico Regionale. **Taormina**, in a beautiful setting with views of Mount Etna, has another ancient Greek theatre. See also Valle dei Templi (➤ 40–41).

www.palermotourism.com; www.insicilia.it
🚩 140 E2 (Palermo) 🚢 Ferry from Naples or Genoa to Palermo or from Reggio di Calabria to Messina ✈ International flights to Palermo or Catania 🛈 Palermo: Piazza Castelnuovo 34 (☎ 091 605 8111). Piazza Armerina: Via Cavour 1 (☎ 0935 680 201). Siracusa: Via S Sebastiano 43 and 47 (☎ 0931 481 200). Taormina: Palazzo Corvaja, Corso Umberto I (☎ 0942 23 243)

Index

Acknowledgements

The Automobile Association wishes to thank the following photographers, companies and picture libraries for their assistance in the preparation of this book. Abbreviations for the picture credits are as follows – (t) top; (b) bottom; (l) left; (r) right; (c) centre; (AA) AA World Travel Library

4l Accademia Bridge, Venice, AA/A Mockford & N Bonnetti; **4c** Colosseum, Rome, AA/A Kouprianoff; **4r** Piazza C Alberti, market, Cagliari, AA/C Sawyer; **5l** San Gimignano, AA/S McBride; **5c** Grand Canal, Venice, AA/S McBride; **6/7** Accademia Bridge, Venice, AA/A Mockford & N Bonnetti; **10** Carnival Mask, Venice, AA/D Miterdiri; **12** Aeroplane landing, Marco Polo Airport, Venice, AA/C Sawyer; **13** Mobi Wonder ferry, Livorno, AA/T Harris; **15** Livorno, AA/T Harris; **16** Telephone boxes, Tuscany, AA/T Harris; **18/19** Policeman, Amalfi, AA/M Jourdan; **20/21** Colosseum, Rome, AA/A Kouprianoff; **22** Sistine Chapel ceiling, Rome, AA/S McBride; **22/23** St Peter's Basilica, Rome, AA/A Kouprianoff; **23t** Piazza San Pietro, Rome, AA/D Miterdiri; **23b** Sign for Vatican Museums, Rome, AA/S McBride; **24/25** Accademia Bridge by night, Venice, AA/A Mockford & N Bonnetti; **25** Ca'Rezzonico, Grand Canal, Venice, AA/C Sawyer; **26** Villa Rufolo in Ravello, AA/M Jourdan; **26/27** Sorrento, AA/C Sawyer; **28/29** Duomo, Milan, AA/C Sawyer; **28** Spires on Milan's Duomo, AA/M Jourdan; **29** Statues outside Milan's Duomo, AA/M Jourdan; **30/31t** Colosseum, Rome, AA/S McBride; **30/31b** Roman Forum, Rome, AA/A Kouprianoff; **32** Head of Madonna by Lippi, Uffizi Gallery, Florence, AA; **32/33** Inner Court, Uffizi Gallery, Florence, AA/C Sawyer; **33** The Holy Family by Michelangelo, Uffizi Gallery, Florence, AA/S McBride; **34t** Piazza San Marco, Venice, AA/A Mockford & N Bonnetti; **34b** Piazza San Marco by night, Venice, AA/A Mockford & N Bonnetti; **35** Basilica San Marco, AA/S McBride; **36** Statue, House of the Faun, Pompeii, AA/M Jourdan; **36/37** Ruins at Pompeii, AA/M Jourdan; **37** Mount Vesuvius, AA/A Souter; **38** Mausoleo di Galla Placidia, Ravenna, AA/A Souter; **38/39** Basilica de S Vitale, Ravenna, AA/A Souter; **40/41** Valle dei Templi, Agrigento, AA/C Sawyer; **41** Temple at Valle dei Templi, Agrigento, AA/C Sawyer; **42/43** Piazza C Alberti, market, Cagliari, AA/C Sawyer; **43** View towards Vernazza, AA/A Souter; **46** Casello Sforzesco, Milan, AA/P Bennett; **46/47** Castello Sforzesco Church, AA/M Jourdan; **48/49** Galleria Vittorio Emanuele, Milan, AA/C Sawyer; **49** Santa Maria della Grazie, Milan, AA/M Jourdan; **50/51** Castello di Sarre, AA/C Sawyer; **51** Statue of Stradivarius, Cremona, AA/A Mockford & N Bonnetti; **52/53** Cannero Riviera, Lago Maggiore, AA/A Mockford & N Bonnetti; **53** Stresa, Lago Maggiore, AA/A Mockford & N Bonnetti; **54/55** Portovenere, AA/A Souter; **56** Rococo Villa Reale di Stupinigi, Turin, AA/A Souter; **57** Duomo, Treviso, AA/C Sawyer; **58/59** Ca d'Oro, view down Grand Canal, Venice, AA/S McBride; **59t** Galleria Accademia, Venice, AA/A Mockford & N Bonnetti; **59b** Ca d'oro, Venice, AA/C Sawyer; **60** Santi Giovanni e Paolo, from Campanile, Venice, AA/S McBride; **60/61** Santi Giovanni e Paolo, Venice, AA/S McBride; **61** The Crucifixion, by Tintoretto, Scuola di San Rocco, Venice, AA/D Miterdiri; **62/63** Fontana del Nettuno, Bologna, AA/C Sawyer; **63** Arca di S Domenico, Bologna, AA/C Sawyer; **64/65** Ferrara, AA/C Sawyer; **66** Piazza Cermenati, Lago Lecco, AA/M Jourdan; **67** Baptistery, Palma, AA/A Souter; **69/70** San Signori, Treviso, AA/C Sawyer; **70/71** Arena, Verona, AA/A Souter; **72** Pizza eaters, AA/C Sawyer; **73** Arezzo, AA/K Paterson; **74/75** Basilica de S Maria del Fiore, Florence, AA/K Paterson; **75** Michelangelo's David, Galleria dell'Accademia, Florence, AA/S McBride; **76** Museo Nazionale del Bargello, Florence, AA/S McBride; **76/77** Palazzo Medici-Riccardi, Florence, AA/C Sawyer; **77** Palazzo Pitti, Florence, AA/S McBride; **78/79t** Ponte Vecchio, Florence, AA/S McBride; **78/79b** Ponte Vecchio, Florence, AA/T Harris; **79** San Marco Church, Florence, AA/S McBride; **80** Basilica di San Croce, Florence, AA/C Sawyer; **80/81** Santa Maria del Carmine, Florence, AA/C Sawyer; **81** Santa Maria Novella Church, Florence, AA/T Harris; **82** Arezzo Monthly Market, AA/T Harris; **84/85c** Panel depicting St Francis, Assisi, AA/K Paterson; **84/85b** Assisi, AA/P Davies; **85** Madonna del Calcinaio, Cortona, AA/C Sawyer; **86** Portoferraio, Elba, AA/K Paterson; **86/87** Palazzo dei Consoli, Gubbio, AA/T Harris; **88** Duomo, Orvieto, AA/K Paterson; **88/89** Leaning Tower of Pisa, AA/C Sawyer; **90** Pistoia, AA/K Paterson; **90/91** San Gimignano, AA/K Paterson; **92** Torre del Mangia, AA/C Sawyer; **92/93** Duomo, Siena, AA/T Harris; **93** Campello san Clitunno, Spoleto, AA/K Paterson; **94** Palazzo Ducale, Urbino, AA/C Sawyer; **94/95** Todi, AA/K Paterson; **95** Ruins of Roman Theatre, Volterra, AA/R Ireland; **96** Badia Fiorentian, Forence, AA/C Sawyer; **97** Ostia Antica, AA/C Sawyer; **98** Bocca della Verita, Santa Maria in Cosmedin, Rome, AA/J Holmes; **98/99** Piazza del Campidoglio, Rome, AA/A Kouprianoff; **100** Ponte Sant'Angelo, AA/S McBride; **100/101** Bernini's Rape of Prosperine, Galleria Borghese, AA/D Miterdiri; **101** Palazzo Altemps, AA/S McBride; **102** Nazionale d'Arte Antica, Palazzo Barberini, Rome, AA/P Wilson; **102/103** Palazzo Doria, AA/P Wilson; **103** Pantheon, Rome, AA/S McBride; **104** Fontana di Trevi, AA/C Sawyer; **104/105** Trinita dei Monti, Rome, AA/C Sawyer; **106** San Clemente, Rome, AA/S McBride; **107t** San Laterano, Rome, AA/S McBride; **107b** Santa Maria Maggiore, AA/S McBride; **108/109** L'Aquila, AA/C Sawyer; **110/111** Amphitheatre, Ostia Antica, AA/S McBride; **111** Villa Adriana, Tivoli, AA/S Mcbride; **112** Piazza Santa Maria della Pace, Rome, AA/A Kouprianoff; **113** Costa Smeralda, AA/C Sawyer; **114** Castel Nuovo, Naples, AA/M Jourdan; **114/115** Palazzo Reale, Naples, AA/M Jourdan; **115** Castle Sant Elmo, AA/M Jourdan; **116/117** Capodimonte Gardens, AA/M Jourdan; **118** Wine bottles, AA/A Souter; **118/119** Basilica di San Nicola, AA/C Sawyer; **119** Basilica di San Nicola, Bari, AA/C Sawyer; **120/121** Santa Maria del Isola, Tropea, AA/A Souter; **121** Castel del Monte, Puglia, AA/C Sawyer; **122/123** Sasso Caveoso, AA/A Souter; **123** Doric Temple of Neptune, Paestum, AA/A Souter; **124** Reggio, AA/C Sawyer; **124/125** Costa Smeralda, AA/C Sawyer; **126/127** Mount Etna, Taormina, AA/C Sawyer; **127** Cefalu, AA/C Sawyer

Every effort has been made to trace the copyright holders, and we apologise in advance for any accidental errors. We would be happy to apply the corrections in the following edition of this publication.

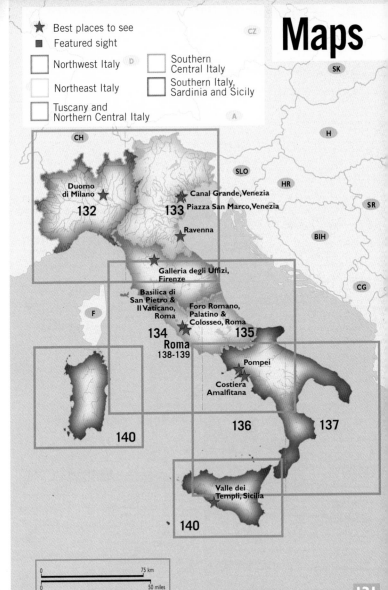

Maps

★ Best places to see
■ Featured sight

Northwest Italy

Northeast Italy

Tuscany and
Northern Central Italy

Southern
Central Italy

Southern Italy,
Sardinia and Sicily

CZ

SK

D

A

H

CH

SLO

HR

SR

BIH

CG

F

Duomo
di Milano ★

132

Canal Grande, Venezia

133 Piazza San Marco, Venezia

Ravenna

Galleria degli Uffizi,
Firenze

Basilica di
San Pietro &
Il Vaticano,
Roma

134

Roma
138-139

Foro Romano,
Palatino &
Colosseo, Roma

135

Pompei

Costiera
Amalfitana

136

137

140

Valle dei
Templi, Sicilia

140

0 _____ 75 km
0 _____ 50 miles

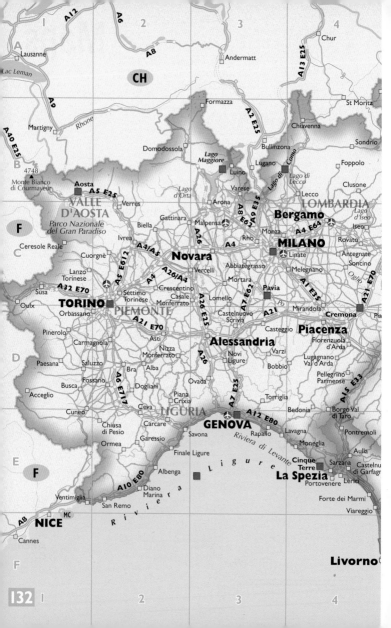

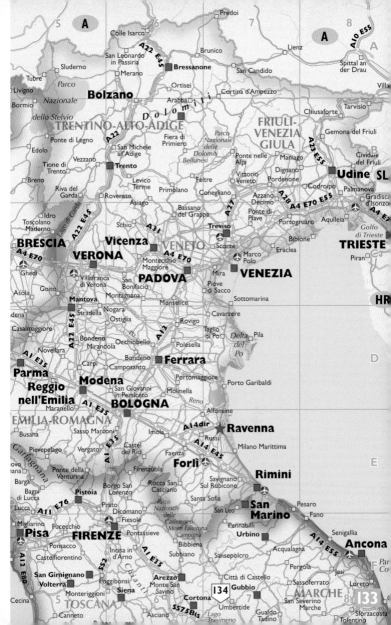

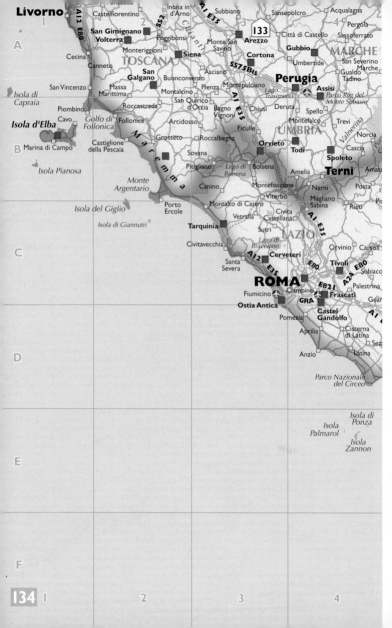

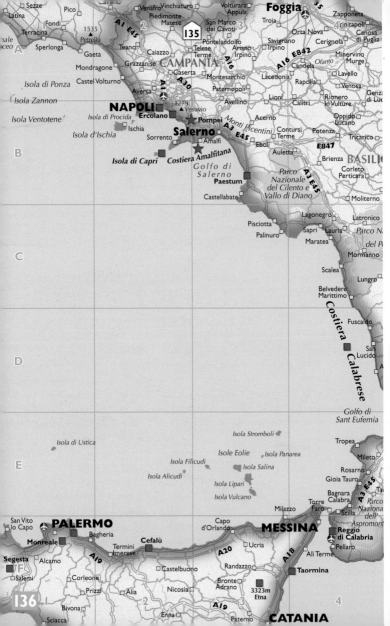

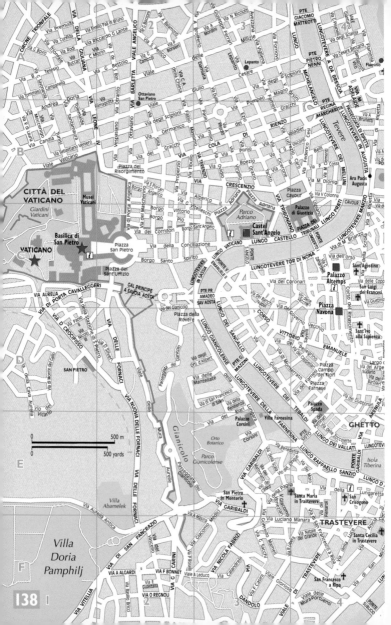

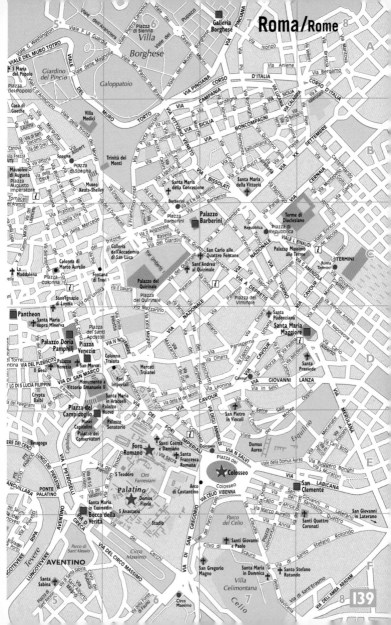

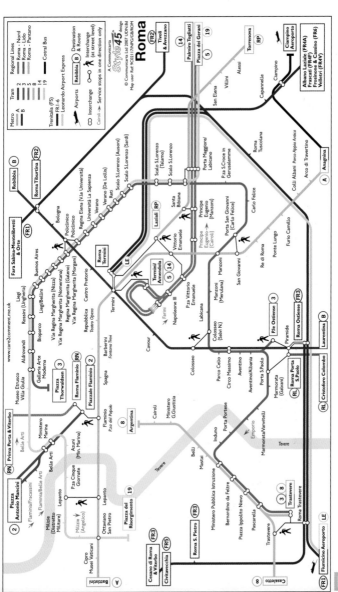

Notes